In the Country

Angela Rippon, Phil Drabble, Bernard Price,
Ted Moult, Tom Weir, Elizabeth Eyden, Richard Mabey,
Joe Henson and Gordon Beningfield

Edited by Peter Crawford

M

First published 1980 by Macmillan London Limited
London and Basingstoke

Associated companies in Delhi, Dublin,
Hong Kong, Johannesburg, Lagos, Melbourne,
New York, Singapore and Tokyo

Published by arrangement with the British Broadcasting Corporation

Printed in Great Britain by
Butler & Tanner Ltd, Frome and London

British Library Cataloguing in Publication Data

In the Country.
    1. Country life – Great Britain
    2. Natural history – Great Britain
    I. Crawford, Peter
    941'.00973'4   DA667

ISBN 0–333–29325–8

Contents

The Armchair Countryside

PETER CRAWFORD

Television has played a large part in the popularisation of the countryside. Programmes about wildlife and the great outdoors are enjoyed by all kinds of viewers who find them entertaining, escapist and, above all, informative. For many of us these 'television safaris' are as good as the real thing – often better. We see more and in greater comfort, and nature is revealed and explained with more clarity and ingenuity than we could ever enjoy in the wild. We are armchair naturalists exploring the countryside without ever needing to go there.

Most of us, either by choice or necessity, live in towns. It's probably just as well that we do since there are now so many of us, and the congested urban way of life that we have devised for ourselves has considerable attractions and compensations. In fact some people feel ill at ease in the country – open spaces literally give them agoraphobia – and it can indeed be an inhospitable place, unsheltered from the elements and the changing seasons. For others it is this exposure to the natural world which is the greatest appeal of the countryside.

It is only two or three generations since many families in Britain were country born and bred – earning a living from the soil or practising a country craft or profession that was very much part of the economy of Britain. Then towns were the curiosities, places to visit on a day off, in search of recreation and a new tempo of life. It is a truism that the roles of town and country have now been reversed, but what is surprising is how quickly we have lost the trappings of our country origins – the skills and crafts, the basic knowledge and understanding of nature, and often the attitudes and values that were the life-blood of a country way of life. Perhaps it is to our credit that we can adapt so rapidly to a new way of life and make the best of it. But it is now a century and more since the great shift of population to the towns took place and we have come to appreciate even more what we've been missing. Like an unrequited love the country beckons us back.

I

But if we all went back, even for a weekend, there would probably be no countryside left to tell the tale. Our very numbers would have spoiled what we had travelled to see. Heaven knows what would happen if we all decided to stay and set up some kind of self-sufficient cell in the country, growing our own food and living a rural life. Theoretically we could have half an acre each, if it was all ours to share out, but many of us would have a rough time, for much of the British landscape is unproductive and best simply for looking at. Greener though the grass may seem out there, I doubt if we could survive.

What then do we want from our countryside? Food, timber, minerals and water apart, it must be some kind of spiritual reassurance. The country is a retreat to which we can escape both physically and mentally; a standard against which we can measure the successes and failures of our other world; a barometer of civilisation. For Wordsworth it was the Lake District; for Constable, the banks of the Stour in Suffolk. For others it is the flight of the golden eagle above a Scottish glen, or the call of the curlew. At a more human level, it might be the ring of the blacksmith's anvil or the smell of a traditional leather tannery. For all of us, being 'in the country' means something different.

In the television series we've tried to reflect these different things that we expect from the countryside. One of the best ways of doing this is through the interests and opinions of people who live and work there; through them we can share a view of the country which is informed, practical and sympathetic. It is all too easy to approach country matters from an urban point of view – to be over-romantic or patronising or, worse still, to overlook the fact that there are a lot of people who work in our countryside and care for it as they've always done.

During the last three years, I have collected together a group of people such as this, who have in addition the ability to communicate their enthusiasm and concern for country matters. They have met regularly to take part in our BBC-2 series *In the Country* and have brought to the television screen a gentle blend of knowledge, opinion and good humour – a weekly breath of fresh country air to take us through the long winter evenings. From the appreciative reactions we've had to the series, it's clear that this personal style of presenting country topics has been welcomed by town and country viewers alike. In portraying the countryside and country life, we have tried to be realistic and honest while not forgetting the essential qualities of charm, colour and space that make the British countryside so appealing.

It falls to *Angela Rippon* to hold together our select and highly individual group of country personalities. Her great charm and professionalism bring out the best in us. She has a true understanding and concern for country matters, and an inquiring mind which questions why life in the country is so different and why it has become important to so many people. Angela would not claim to be a naturalist or an expert on rural life, but she has a unique ability to draw from her guests, and the other country people she meets on the programme, an informative and entertaining account of whatever topic we have chosen to feature on the air. In this book we have a chance to hear more about Angela's own country life, to which she rushes back from her other very public existence in the television centres at London, Bristol and elsewhere up and down the country. I know that she and her husband, Chris, have a great affinity with the countryside and its wildlife, and I'm sure that, through her association with the programme and the people in it, she has discovered new aspects that have brought additional enjoyment to the spare time they spend together in their own special part of Devon.

Our other contributors – both to the television series and the book – come from every corner of the country. *Phil Drabble* and his wife Jess live in Staffordshire, surrounded by the forests and farmland of the Midlands. Beyond is the Black Country where Phil was brought up amid the potteries and collieries, which have their own brand of enthusiasm for dogs and ferrets, racing and poaching. Phil has done it all; he's a cunning countryman whose wit and wisdom I greatly respect.

Phil Drabble shows Angela Rippon one of the pheasant poults that run wild in his private woodland which he manages as a nature reserve for all kinds of wildlife.

3

A far cry from the Black Country is *Bernard Price's* beloved Sussex where, cradled between the North and South Downs and mellowed by the sea, country life has an air of gentleness and antiquity that Bernard captures in his descriptions of the rural crafts and traditions of a bygone age.

Down in the South West *Elizabeth Eyden* works to promote the interests of nature conservation and particularly of the World Wildlife Fund, in an area which we have come to associate with everything that is worth preserving about the countryside. It is here, perhaps more than anywhere else, that the greatest tension is felt between the need for more space to grow food and trees and the demands of the millions of enthusiasts who want to enjoy the special beauty and atmosphere of this corner of Britain.

There's more space in the Cotswolds – great open prairies of barley and wheat on the high windswept plateau. This is not everybody's ideal landscape but *Joe Henson*, who farms a thousand acres of it, has made it his home. As a reminder of how farming used to be, Joe also runs a farm park there, where visitors can see his collection of rare and unusual breeds of farm animals which, until the modern revolution in agriculture, were the mainstays of the farmyard. He writes nostalgically of their virtues, and is hopeful for their future.

Another farmer well known to viewers of *In the Country* is *Ted Moult*. He is a rare breed himself, combining a mixture of good humour and down-to-earth common sense. Ted farms on the border between Derbyshire and Leicestershire. His farmhouse, on the edge of a valley, has an uninterrupted and breathtaking view of open countryside. Since he moved there, his large family has grown up to see enormous changes in the agricultural scene around them. No longer does Ted milk cows that graze on green pastures; instead his fields are planted with strawberries and other crops that meet the needs of today's population. But for Ted a spade is still a spade; both he and Joe Henson, in their own different ways, are modern men of the soil.

One way to earn a living from the countryside, or at least to become involved in it, is to paint, photograph or write about it. For centuries writers, poets and artists have extolled its virtues, cherished its enduring qualities or mourned its demise. *In the Country* has its own happy band of authors and artists who reflect their feeling for the countryside in words and pictures. *Richard Mabey* lives in the Home Counties and, as a naturalist and ecologist, highlights the changes to the natural world brought about by the increasing demands we make on it. *Tom Weir*, three hundred miles away on the banks of Loch Lomond, echoes the same theme from the point of view of someone who especially values the wilder parts of Britain – the province of the walker and birdwatcher. And only half an hour from the centre of London, in a village that seems unchanged since the feudal days of the squire, *Gordon Beningfield* captures the classic English countryside in pencil, watercolour, and oil. From

4

In the Country visits the Royal Agricultural Show. Elizabeth Eyden, Angela Rippon, Ted Moult and Joe Henson with a prize-winning Polled British White bull.

butterflies to old gateposts, from shepherds' bells to cobwebs, he finds delight in the simple, familiar sights on his doorstep. No wonder he admires the work of Thomas Bewick. Gordon adds his own pen and ink vignettes to the written contributions of his friends who join him 'in the country'.

As producer of the television programme, I could not have had a more sincere and entertaining group of people to work with. When exploring rural Britain with them, researching and filming for the series, I could not have wished for better company, or for more stimulating and informed discussion about rural topics. Between them these broadcasters have a wealth of country common sense and a breadth of appreciation and experience that makes them a unique team. In compiling this book, I hope that you too will be able to share their feeling for the countryside and their concern for its future.

Unlike the television programme, the book is intended to be a companion that you can take with you into the country. The advice and information the authors give is based on first-hand experience; the views they hold are very much their own – sometimes they even disagree between themselves. And if, perhaps in the heart of some town or on a dark wet winter's evening, you have a wish to be 'in the country' again, I am sure you will find my friends good company.

At Home —
In the Country

ANGELA RIPPON

The very first time my husband Chris and I set eyes on our house, we knew it was where we wanted to live for the rest of our lives.

Built into the side of a hill, in the centre of a two-acre garden, the cottage looks due south across a wooded valley towards the gentle, bracken-clad hills that mark the very edge of Dartmoor.

That was more than ten years ago when we were quite simply looking for a home in the country. Since then my work has taken me to every major country in the northern hemisphere, and committed me to a see-saw existence where I live only part of my life in Devon and spend the rest working in cities and studios hundreds of miles away.

It would have been so easy to sell up and move to London, to be at the centre of things. But somehow the more exhausting the work and the more demanding the commitments, the more important it is to head my car westwards and escape to my own very private life in the country.

From my office in the Television Centre at Shepherd's Bush in London I have a wonderful view of the car park, the corrugated iron bicycle sheds, the tube station, and the motorway beyond. The only wildlife I'm likely to see (apart from the commuters) are the Beeb's feral cats, and the ubiquitous crows and London sparrows hustling for air space with the aircraft flying in and out of Heathrow.

That precious air space around our cottage is only 247 miles down the motorway, but it might as well be light years away.

My first morning at home after a spell away always begins with the same ritual. I make myself a cup of coffee and, still in my dressing gown, sit at one of the windows to take in the world around me – to note the subtle changes in the colour and shape of the plants in the garden and the trees in the wood; to watch the birds and the squirrels and any other creature that cares to call in the early morning.

6

Even though our garden is crammed with trees that blend across an almost invisible boundary into hundreds of acres of woods and gorse all teeming with bird life, we still have a bird table just a few feet from the back door. All the year round it's stocked with food. I know the experts say that you shouldn't feed birds in the summer, but ours still come looking for the occasional treat of dried fruit or wholemeal bread, and why should we disappoint them?

In the cold months of autumn and winter we build them up with nuts and cheese, bread, bacon rinds, and any scraps we think they might fancy. As a result Dare's Diner must be on the Good Eating Guide for every bird in the neighbourhood, for we're never short of guests.

The blue tits and great tits are the boldest – and the hungriest – and it seems that whenever we look out of a window there's a flash of blue hanging upside down on the nut cage or working its way through the menu on the cold table.

The finches 'cheep' noisily between courses, and always come back for seconds. But they haven't yet persuaded their cousins, the bullfinches, to forsake the shrubbery and join them at the table. Instead the forsythia boughs spring up and down under the weight of their chubby little red and black bodies as they strip the bushes of their succulent buds. So we never have fountains of frothy yellow forsythia in our garden – but the leaves are always beautiful.

Not all the regulars are small birds. A pair of magpies and a fully grown jay come daily to be fed. They were born in nests somewhere in the garden last summer. The parents have moved on, but the babes, recognising a good thing when they see it, have stayed. They're not tame by any means but, like the rest of the birds in the garden, they're certainly not afraid of us and will come when called, or sit in the trees scolding and chattering if they think that we're late with their breakfast. They rarely eat at the table. The jay will fill its crop and beak full of choice cuts, then swoop off, rising and dipping through the orchard, to a sheltered branch in a sycamore tree to eat alone.

As for the magpies – they're such pompous birds on land, puffing out their white shirt-fronts and strutting about with that arrogant, swaggering walk. But their table manners are appalling. They cram tit-bits into their beaks like meat on a kebab skewer, then they bustle off to a flat piece of lawn, or the ridge tiles on one of the outbuildings, to gorge themselves. Sometimes I've seen them land, look about furtively to make sure that no one was watching, then scratch at the lawns to make a small hollow, bury their cache, and then, just as furtively, cover it over with leaves and grass. It all looks very efficient, but I've never seen them come back for a mid-day snack, so either they forget where they've hidden their goodies or someone else beats them to it.

That 'someone' could be one of our squirrels. Not red ones alas – they disappeared years ago – but grey squirrels, the scourge of the forester. I know they're pests, I know that they play havoc with our trees (I only have to look

A love of the countryside and of dogs seems to go together. Here Angela gets to know Phil Drabble's old lurcher called Fly.

at the jagged, distorted crown of our lovely copper beech to be reminded of just how destructive they are) but they're also delightful to watch and I've lost count of the hours Chris and I have whiled away leaning over the kitchen door, or motionless at a window, charmed by their antics.

Not long after we'd bought the house, I remember we spent a breathless twenty minutes watching a squirrel eating dandelion heads. At that time the garden at the back of the house was a wild tumble of thorn and nettle where the grass had grown, uncut, for nearly three years, and the dandelions cropped a golden harvest in the summer.

They weren't the squashy sort on hollow creamy stalks, but the kind that grow up to ten inches tall with small heads on the end of whippy, dark green stems. The squirrel sat at the base of a stalk, and stretched up, hand over hand, until he reached the flower head, which he bent towards his mouth and snapped off, then let the stalk spring back like a catapult. When he'd cleared a patch around himself, he'd move on to another choice site, all the time getting nearer and nearer the house. Suddenly he stopped dead – and froze. Slowly a shadow slid down the grassy bank as a buzzard circled overhead. For a second the outline of a massive wing tip brushed across his body, blotting out the sun. The bird passed on, the squirrel turned tail, and the spell was broken.

We cursed that we hadn't captured the moment on film, or been able to see him more closely. Since then we've kept binoculars in the kitchen and a camera near to hand. And although our squirrels are now daily visitors, bobbing across the lawns, posing beautifully on rocks amid the alpine garden, and throwing caution to the wind to climb the bird table and sit under its small roof, they never fail to charm and delight me.

Mind you – it's a pity about the trees! And we're literally surrounded by them; silver birch and ash, the sad, struggling elms, beech and sycamore, oak and hawthorn, and many more. The centrepiece of the front garden is a mighty ilex oak, an evergreen that sheds its leaves by the bucketful in the autumn, and throughout the year is a Tower of Babel for the bird population.

That oak tree is like a fourteen-storey block of flats. It's always full of birds roosting, nesting, passing through, or just meeting friends. It's a look-out tower from which they plot the position of the two family cats and set up a clarion of warning calls once they're spotted, and a perfect observation post for watching the bird table.

And while they watch it – I watch them. Blackbirds stride across the lawns, heads cocked, looking with bright eyes for a juicy worm to sandwich between chunks of bread. Song and mistle thrushes stuff themselves fit to burst with holly berries off the huge ornamental trees in the shrubbery. Robins dash across invisible boundaries on snatch-and-grab raids in each other's territory, and the independent little Jenny Wren busies around with tail in the air and a song on the wind. Pied and grey wagtails dip and tip on those frail little legs, a green or greater spotted woodpecker greedily buries its beak in an ant-hill or the bark of a tree, and buzzards mew and soar on thermals, wings motionless and head gyrating in search of a warm, fresh meal.

Because I can't look out of the window and take in the view on every morning of the week like any normal housewife, the change from one season to another is somehow more marked. It's a bit like watching one of those films in which the camera has taken only a single picture every few hours, so that when you run the film at normal speed you see a bud burst, stretch into full bloom and die in a matter of seconds, instead of days.

So it is with the view from my windows.

The four seasons paint their different-coloured brushstrokes across the landscape, turning the leaves and the bracken from pale translucent green to the gold and burgundy of autumn. It may take a year to happen in reality – but for me the whole process is telescoped into a month.

Each winter, for a few days, everything is soundproofed by a thick, sparkling duvet of snow. Then come the daffodils, tumbling down through the orchard and bursting like pools of bright sunshine on to the banks of the old railway track at the bottom of the garden. One day the trees are bare, black fingers on the skyline – the next they're hung with fragile soft green leaves that filter the first sunshine of spring. And in no time at all the rich, brown leafmould on the floor of the wood is silently and invisibly nudged out of the way by thousands of tiny, sharp green spears which push and grow and blossom into a cloud of bluebells.

At the height of summer the buddleia and sedums sprout a double crop of bloom: flowers and butterflies. And then, with the stealth of a bitten apple turning brown, the beech leaves go from summer green to autumn gold, and the bracken deepens to mahogany in the short, sunfilled days of early autumn. We stop cutting flowers, and start winter pruning. The mahonia throws out its brash yellow flowers in defiance of December, and we wait for the inevitable winter gales to take their toll of yet another crop of trees that are too old and too dry.

That first cup of coffee, lingered over and frequently topped up, gives me time to take it all in. The birds, the seasons, the weather, the 'state' of my private world. Then I'm ready to face the rest of the day.

That invariably means donning jodhpurs, boots and a sweater to exercise my horse. Katie (or, to give her her proper name, Extra Time) is stabled just a mile or so from the house at a livery yard that backs straight on to open moorland. For at least an hour we can both enjoy the total freedom of speed and space over some of the finest riding country in Britain, with only the sheep and moorland ponies for company.

From time to time we combine what skill and courage we can muster to compete in a hunter trial, an event or a showjumping competition. On those occasions it's nice not to be a 'personality'. I'm just another competitor who'll be judged, not on my name, but on how successfully I ride the course.

I suppose, if I really think about it, it's the ordinariness of my life in the country that is so appealing. When I'm 'on show' in front of the cameras my hair, make-up and clothes must be just so. But if I choose to nip into Tavistock to do some shopping straight from the stable, no one minds that I'm still in jodhpurs and wellies, wrapped in a warm anorak with my hair tucked away under a scarf and my face having a day off from the paintwork.

On market days I can guarantee that, even though the shopping should only take half an hour, I'll spend at least an hour catching up on gossip and news with friends. For in a small town like Tavy (as we always refer to it) it's impossible to walk a hundred yards without meeting someone you know. And while Angela Rippon of the BBC News might be expected to know all about the state of the British economy, the day's events in Parliament and the world's latest crisis spot, Mrs Christopher Dare of Tavistock can be more concerned with the newest baby, the cost of hay and the date of the next Country Dance evening in the Town Hall.

The River Tavy runs through the centre of the town. Eventually it meets the River Tamar which rushes out to Plymouth Sound in a confusion of cross tides and to the English Channel beyond the breakwater. But a mile or so from Tavistock, at the aptly named Double Waters, it crashes through granite and plantations of pine to meet 'our' river, the Walkham, which flows through the valley below our home.

Chris and I spend a lot of our time together walking. We both love the sights, the sounds and the smells of the countryside; the pleasure of being able to say 'Oh, look at that', and share the moment with someone special.

Walking the dogs is a good excuse for going out – though we would anyway. Until recently we had two dogs. Muffin, our black and white King Charles cross, who's ten, but still chases four ways at once like a puppy. And Plod, my beloved old basset who died last year aged sixteen. Our regular route would take us from the garden gate, down a narrow sloping track through the woods to the river, shaded by oak and sycamore that have stood, it seems, for centuries. While Muffin would chase a favoured stick through bramble, bog and the deepest fastest stretch of the river, Plod would amble at his own sedate pace, stopping now and then to stand four-square and solid on those chunky, cabriole legs of his, with his magnificent head held high, sniffing at the air, and his larger-than-life ears trailing in the mud.

We once spent twenty minutes watching what I so desperately wanted to be an otter, but which quite clearly was just another wild mink. And after weeks of smelling Mr Fox in the early morning dew, I saw him at last walk out in front of me – so close I could have touched him – before padding off into the shadows.

Occasionally the cats, Solo and Fluffs, deign to join us, picking their way daintily over the cleanest ground and suddenly showing off with a wild explosion of energy that shoots them up the tallest trees, from which they look down with impudent lofty independence.

As I write this we're waiting on a new arrival – a baby basset. How he'll react to our established menagerie, our woods and river, I don't know. But I hope he'll grow to love them as much as we do.

At times, I know, my city-loving friends find it difficult to understand how I can happily swop elegant shoes for wellies, fashionable clothes for sweaters and jeans, carefully dressed hair for ear-hugging woolly hats and headscarves. They see me as something of a schizophrenic, equally at home with both lives and living each independently of the other.

I know that one day I'll have to be content with just one of those lives, but for the time being, living in the country keeps me sane for working in the crazy world of television. And it's my life in television that makes me more aware of, and more grateful for, the life I lead 'in the country'.

Lurchers, Terriers and Poachers

PHIL DRABBLE

Owd Austin was not the man to tangle with. He was one of the most powerful men I have ever seen but he was such a merry fellow that the stubble on his chin and cheeks only added to his benign expression. This was accentuated by his grin. In top and bottom jaw he had not one row of teeth, but two. The slightest suspicion of a snarl would have made him as sinister as a crocodile but, since he was always chuckling with merriment, I remember him only with the greatest affection.

Austin's mother was not an imaginative woman, so when she had twins she couldn't think what to call them and went to the priest for advice. He said that they should have biblical names and, since it was very unlucky for a child to be called his brother's name by mistake, suggested that one be called Augustin Daniel and the other Daniel Augustin. Then if anyone got mixed up as to which was which, they would still address them correctly. This proved of inestimable value in later life. They grew up to look identical and when one wanted to go poaching the other had a night in the local pub. If a keeper caught a glimpse of one of them out after a pheasant he was wise to keep his distance – the description 'not a man to tangle with' was no exaggeration. The prudent thing to do was to get moral support from the local bobby and call at the house, but prudence does not always gain the day; the unbreakable alibi was that it couldn't have been whichever one was seen because the customers in the local would vouch for the fact that 'he' was propping up the bar all evening.

Although I never knew Daniel Augustin very well, I served my apprentice-ship with Augustin Daniel. He was known all over the Black Country of Staffordshire as 'the 'erb mon' because he hawked his sage and thyme and other herbs for many miles around. He grew these in a seven-acre field right on the edge of three large farms. Not surprisingly, the herbs made perfect cover for game, and the pheasants and partridge from all around took refuge there whenever they were disturbed.

From the age of ten, my inseparable companion was Mick, a mongrel bull-and-fox terrier which was famous for miles around as a ratting dog. He was a wonderfully biddable little dog and his tastes were not confined to rats; almost anything that moved was fair game in his book. So, most Sunday mornings Austin would go down to his herb field with his muzzle loader and I would go for a walk around the farms across his boundary. Mick busy-bodied around, probing every tussock and bramble and, purely by coincidence of course, we always 'happened' to be working towards Austin's field. Quarry we disturbed flew or ran for refuge there, only to be greeted by a blast from Austin's gun. And, since he was on his own ground, he wasn't poaching.

When landowners noticed me walking round with the dog, it never occurred to them that there was any link between Austin and me. I was a polite, respectable, well-scrubbed little lad – the last chap in the world to get mixed up with anything disreputable. When I couldn't find anything else to drive across him, I wandered over to join old Austin who then lent me his gun to have a pot at anything I could find, from starlings to rabbits.

That old terrier was the light of my eyes. My father was a doctor and many of his patients were farmers, so there was always a welcome for me to take a ferret and catch as many rats as we could. I spent a great deal of my holidays with a professional rat-catcher called Hairy Kelly, who had forgotten more about the intimate habits of rats than modern pest-destruction officers will ever know. He taught me to look for clues like cobwebs over holes and greasy streaks up the corners of walls where the rats climbed up to get among the rafters. I knew the significance of well-padded rat runs and could almost think like a rat, so that I could project with accuracy where to place the dog to cut off the rats' retreat when my ferret bolted them from their holes.

By all the rules, I should have been put off ratting for keeps before I reached my teens. One day I was on a farm which had a low bank along the edge of the rick yard, with an iron-railing fence on top of the bank. Rats, working in the ricks at night, had made warrens like rabbit burrows in the earth bank below the fence. Starting at the end nearest the ricks, I put the ferret down a hole, hoping to drive the rats gradually towards the far end so that, when they were at last forced to bolt into the open, there would be every chance for the dog to catch them before they reached another sanctuary. We didn't get that far. Instead of going down the hole towards the main bank, as I expected, the ferret disappeared towards the dead end of the bank, which was only a few feet away. And there she stayed.

I hung around, seeing nothing and hearing nothing, even when I put my ear to the ground. Getting fed-up after about half an hour, I stuck my hand down the hole where she had disappeared, but could feel nothing. Then I noticed a hole, almost stuffed with straw, at the very tip of the bank. I shoved my hand up it, to see if I could feel the ferret – and she bit me. Or I thought it was the ferret, but I couldn't be sure. All I knew was that something had me firmly by the ball of the thumb and I couldn't pull my hand out.

Kids of twelve are not so tough. Or I wasn't. I screamed and yelled blue murder till a farm labourer came running up, and rushed off again to get a spade and dug away the bank.

It wasn't the ferret that had bitten me; it was the father and mother of all giant rats. Apparently he had been trying to escape when the ferret had laid hold of his backside and hung on. The hole was too narrow for him to turn and fight the ferret, who splayed her legs to hold the rat fast, until I literally put my thumb in his jaw for him to take it out on me. His top jaw had split my thumb nail and his lower jaw had pierced the ball of my thumb until the teeth met on the bone. He was as game as a fighting cock, for he died with his teeth locked so that the labourer had to dig him out and get the ferret off the other end before he could unhook his jaws and free my thumb.

I suppose there is a dash of primitive hunting instinct deep down in most of us. I know that, as a naturalist, I experience much the same sort of thrill whether I'm stalking a shy bird with a pair of field glasses or trying to predict where a rat or rabbit will bolt from the ferret and placing the dog to cut off his retreat. There is a very thin line between the dedicated, scientific ornithologist chasing swans across the surface of a lake to fit rings on their legs for research, and learning all you can about the habits of rats so that you can outwit and capture them. If I say anything on the air or write an article about fox hunting or shooting, I get a wastepaper-basketful of letters, but nobody complains that I enjoy the sport of ratting.

An actor friend of mine, who had landed a plum part in a series about the countryside, once asked me to take him ratting because, he said, he knew little about the country and wanted to get under the skin of the part he was to play. I had two very good Stafford bull terriers at the time, each of which had killed over a hundred rats on a good day and a thousand in a year, and I took my friend to a poultry farm where I knew there were a lot.

We were doing fine, the dogs had caught between thirty and forty, when I noticed my visitor was standing in the middle of a barn with rats running all over his feet. Having spent so much time ratting, it was second nature to me to pull my socks over the turn-ups of my trousers and I hadn't noticed that he had neglected such an elementary precaution. 'Put your socks over your trousers, Norman,' I said, 'or you'll have a rat run up your leg if he's hard pressed for an escape route.' The result is one of my most vivid memories, although it happened years ago. His eyes glazed, his face went white, and I believe he was airborne, putting neither foot to ground, for the next twenty seconds. He wasn't much of a sport for he never came again.

For some time in the fifties I had a marvellous lemon-eyed Stafford bitch whose prowess was famous for miles around. Then tragedy struck.

It was before the days when pups were automatically inoculated against distemper and hepatitis and she was bitten so often that the inevitable happened: she contracted jaundice and died. I was so heartbroken that in spite of effective modern vaccines, I said I would never put another dog at risk again, and I never have. I decided to catch the long-eared instead of the long-tailed, and brought Dinah, a whippet lurcher pup.

Her mother was a pure-bred whippet and her father a cross between a whippet and a long-legged terrier; she looked like a sturdy whippet as there was three-quarters whippet blood in her veins. She shared our lives for the next fourteen years and nobody will ever have a more faithful, intelligent and gentle little dog.

She was marvellous for ferreting rabbits because I didn't even need to net the holes. She would creep as delicately as a cat along the leeward side of a hedge and stop, with questioning paw raised, when she thought there was a rabbit at home. I didn't have to say anything but just waved an imperious hand and she melted away to the other side of the hedge while I put the ferret down a hole. Her ears were rather large and she waved them in all directions like a radar scanner, listening for the telltale rumble of a rabbit moving away from the ferret underground. Wherever it bolted, she was waiting to forestall it, catching it full toss as neatly as a wicket-keeper. If one bolted out on my side, she nipped through the hedge and set off, scooping and retrieving it unless it had got too big a start.

But what we both enjoyed best was a walk through a tussocky meadow on a frosty winter morning, when rabbits love to lie out in the open. Although there was so little terrier blood in her, her nose was as sensitive as a pointer and she would mark a rabbit, freeze, and await instructions. It was then my job to predict which way the rabbit would try to escape so that I could intercept it and choose the longest run in the open, to give the dog the best chance.

One of the fringe benefits of having an outstanding working dog is that it is an open introduction to scores of country characters who might otherwise be shy of strangers. Through Dinah I grew friendly with Bert Gripton who had bred her. Bert had been breeding and working terriers for years – it was nothing to him to have between twenty and thirty in his kennel.

He turned out regularly with the local fox hunt, who paid him a small retainer and a fee for every fox he bolted. If Charlie Fox was unsporting enough to seek sanctuary underground, Bert was sent for and asked to bolt him. The fee that the hunt paid him was peanuts. The important thing to him was that days out hunting were his shop window, for anyone interested could hang around and watch just how well his terriers worked. When they were suitably impressed by a dog's ability, they often asked if he would sell it. 'I'm sorry,' Bert would say. 'This is the best dog in England – but I'll sell you a pup off him.' This often had the effect of inciting the prospective purchaser to make an even bigger offer and the game of hard-to-get increased in tempo until, at last, the 'best dog in England' changed hands at a price even Bert could not refuse. 'When the king is dead, long live the king.' Next week, another 'best dog in England' would be showing his paces.

It was a stirring sight to see Bert dig out a fox, and when I described it to a BBC producer he was visibly impressed. Such fellows are chronically sceptical and believe nothing they hear and only half of what they see; so he asked me to take him for a demonstration.

We picked Bert up at his cottage and he asked us to take him about four miles. When it seemed as if we were in the middle of nowhere, he suddenly told me to leave the car so that we could walk. After half a mile or so, we turned through a gap in the main road hedge and he said, 'Keep your head down. This bloke will let fly with a gun if he sees us. He's very keen on hunting and won't have a fox dug out on his land for a fortune.' It was one o'clock and, although I'd poached most things in my time, I'd never poached a fox in daylight. The producer was even more impressed. At a small earth Bert put a couple of purse nets over holes in the bank and left me to mind them while he took our guest to see the terrier put in, which happened to be Tess, my Dinah's mother. Nothing happened, so he took a small rabbiting spade from his poacher's pocket and started to dig towards where we could hear Tess 'speaking'.

Bert is a tough customer who can make a bulldozer look an amateur when it comes to digging. In two or three minutes, he was down to the bitch's rear end and, grasping the base of her tail, he lifted her gently clear and passed her to me to hold. She had driven the fox up a blind hole where he could back up and present a set of lethal fangs to repel intruders. Tess had wisely stopped six inches short and barked to help the boss locate her.

The business end of a defiant fox offers no obvious hand-holds but Bert produced a stick about a foot long and as thick as a broomstick. He waved it about an inch from the fox's nose so that, striking with the speed of an adder, the fox gripped and held on with bulldog tenacity. The instant he was preoccupied, Bert leaned forward, grabbed him by the scruff of the neck and heaved him out to be dumped unceremoniously in a sack. It was one continuous, smooth movement, as deft as any conjuror – but it takes a lot of guts to extract a defiant fox from his hole with bare hands, however dexterous one may be. We scraped the earth back into the hole, camouflaged it with fallen leaves and departed, heads down, the way we had come before 'the bloke could let fly with his gun'.

Bert Gripton, the terrier-man, who may have as many as twenty or thirty terriers in his kennel at one time – each 'the best dog in England'.

The stories about Bert's wizardry with foxes are legion, but the one I like best, which may be apocryphal though I believe it to be true, is about the time he fell out with the local hunt. He had been 'lifting' foxes from a neighbouring hunt whose master complained in no uncertain terms, so his local hunt had no alternative but to sack him. As a result they had nineteen consecutive blank days because Bert went the night before to the place where the meet was advertised and bolted or 'removed' foxes from all the earths in the area. So they had to take him on again.

When myxomatosis came and it seemed that Dinah's rabbiting days were drawing to a close, I decided to get a 'proper' lurcher.

No rural topic raises temperatures higher than the subject of hare coursing. Opponents of the sport are chronically addicted to emotive phrases about 'live' hare coursing, though it is difficult to imagine how anyone could course hares that were not alive. Addicts of the sport point out that greyhounds have been selectively bred for centuries as sprint animals so that either they catch their hare in a matter of seconds or their speed fades and the quarry escapes. There is no question of hounding it to exhaustion as happens with beagling and some other sports.

The greyhound's superior speed does not guarantee a catch. It can overtake a hare so fast that the hare only has to jink, or dodge, at the last split second to make the dog overshoot it by yards so that it can gain valuable ground towards its chosen refuge before its pursuer catches up again. A judge awards points for each of these turns, and the winner is the dog with the most points when the hare escapes or is caught.

Lurchers are far more efficient at catching hares. They are bred by crossing a pure greyhound or whippet with another breed to give more stamina and intelligence. Ideally, the outcross is a half-bred greyhound so that the resulting lurcher pups have three-quarters pure greyhound blood and one-quarter out-cross. The outcross used depends on the type of country where the dog will work. Deep heather or heavy plough demands a biggish dog with tremendous stamina, for which an outcross of deer hound is ideal. Lurchers with this blood are known as staghound lurchers and, although they will catch a hare on heavy going, they are too cumbersome and cannot turn neatly enough to be very good on small enclosures or little fields.

Phil Drabble's three lurchers – Fly, Spider and Mandy – with his German short-haired pointer called Tick, star of many In the Country *programmes.*

The traditional all-round lurcher is the Smithfield or Norfolk lurcher. In the old days, cattle were fed on the Norfolk marshes and driven by road to Smithfield, feeding along the verges on the way. The cattle drovers used big collies about the size of Old English sheep dogs with long tails and they found that, by crossing these with greyhounds till there was three-quarters greyhound blood, they got far tougher dogs than pure greyhounds, which were still plenty fast enough to catch rabbits and hares to eat on their journeys. They also had coats that would withstand harsh weather and enough intelligence to outwit any country copper who tried to nab them for poaching.

These dogs traditionally lived under gypsy caravans, feeding both themselves and their masters' families, so I bought my first lurcher pup from a 'traveller', who lived in a van and scraped a living by selling scrap and by other less conventional means. I called her Gypsy and she had all the cunning of her kind. She was a born thief and would sit innocently by a visitor at tea, waiting for him to turn his head in conversation. Then, as smooth as a pickpocket, she would nick the sandwich from his plate. It was a family joke to watch her, and her record was to consume three half-sandwiches before the guest caught her and discovered that he had been too engrossed in conversation to notice that he hadn't eaten them himself.

There was a latch on our larder door which didn't always click shut and I've seen her lying, apparently asleep, by the Aga in the kitchen when the larder door did not close tight. She was far too cunning to give the show away, so waited till we left the room before getting up, nipping into the larder and filching anything she could. If we returned to the kitchen before she had had time to eat it, she would lie on it to conceal her booty and pretend to be asleep until the coast was clear again.

She wasn't just a scrounger. She worked for her living as well. I could send her out with a wave of the hand and make her alter direction as accurately as a sheep dog working sheep till she was near where I had seen a hare clap down. When the hare was flushed she chased it, but didn't overshoot it as a greyhound would. She settled down about a yard behind it until it made a fatal mistake, either by checking to go through a hedge or jinking within her reach. There was none of the greyhound's namby-pamby gentility about her. When she caught her hare, she killed it as quickly as a terrier killing a rat. And she was just as effective with foxes.

The sort of gypsy characters who have bred such dogs for generations do not suffer fools gladly and soon dispose of second-raters to the mugs they meet along the way. Survivors like Gypsy would be quite capable of fending for themselves and living off the land if necessity arose, but she was one of the lucky ones, living on Easy Street for many years while I basked in her reflected glory.

The Thatcher

BERNARD PRICE

To the great satisfaction of the thatcher, thatch has become fashionable once more. At the end of the twentieth century no longer is the thatcher a 'man of straw', for it is now possible to obtain a plastic 'thatch'. Most people, however, do seem to prefer the traditional long wheat straw, combed wheat reed or water reed (*Phragmites communis*) obtained in Britain from Kent, Somerset, Suffolk, Norfolk and Scotland.

Reed costs more than straw but it will usually last sixty years, which is likely to span the lifetime of the customer ordering the work. Thatch is more expensive than tiles but its insulation value is enormous; as the old cottagers used to say, 'Warm in winter, cool in summer.' Insurance costs have often penalised the house with thatch, but most thatchers seem to agree that fire risks have always been greatly exaggerated, and reed or straw may anyway be treated with a fireproofing agent before being laid. Not only are we now seeing increasing numbers of old cottages with well-kept thatch but new houses with thatch roofs are also being built. Many churches were once thatched and a few still are.

Today a thatching apprenticeship lasts about four years and, while the principles of thatching are simple enough, the practice is far more difficult. It is also hard work and uncomfortable in bad weather. The oldest of building crafts, thatching has altered but little over the centuries.

If you watch a thatcher at work you will find that he always works from right to left, laying thatch in 'lanes' from eave to ridge, or bottom to top. Long straw is graded and gathered into easily handled bundles called yelms, and eight or ten such bundles are carried on to the roof in a short two-pronged fork, called a yoke, which is usually home-made from a piece of forked hazel. As the thatch is laid the various layers, or 'sways', are held down with setting pins and fixed permanently with lengths of hazel known as spars. The hazel is cut in the coppice, the lengths being split into four. The thatcher usually buys his spars but points them himself. One spar is laid across a layer of thatch, while another is deftly twisted in a way that does not break the fibres but creates a giant hairpin which is pushed right through into the old thatch, thus holding the new layer firmly in place.

Thatching with long straw gives something of a combed hair look, while reed appears to be close-cropped. Straw thatch is trimmed and cut but reed is worked into position with a tool known as a leggat which consists of a square, studded or grooved board with a long handle. Short-handled versions of the leggat are sometimes used for work in difficult corners. Long straw may be recognised by the way it is finished off at the eaves and gables with 'liggers' or cross-spars of hazel in stitch-like patterns. The third form of thatch is combed wheat reed, in which the straw is separated from the ear and left unthreshed. As thatch it has a superior life-span to long straw, and because the reed is laid with the ends exposed it also has a crisper appearance.

At the ridge, dried sedge is often bent across to give a final seal and to provide an opportunity for scalloped or other decoration. Thatchers have always had individual styles and many of them have their own form of decoration or 'signature'.

The renovated weekend cottage of the town-dweller may well prove to have been a major influence in the survival of this great country craft.

A master thatcher and his apprentice working with long straw – a very suitable, and often cheaper, alternative to the more traditional Norfolk reed.

Nature in Trust

ELIZABETH EYDEN

To go northwards from the Polden Hills on to the Somerset Levels is an adventure in time and space. The Levels – the very name evokes the scene – is that area of flat fen-like country interspersed with peat bogs which is bounded to the north-west by the Bristol Channel and the north-east by the Mendips and extends far to the south of the Poldens. There are many heaths and moors on the Levels but these are quite unlike the better known heathlands and moorlands of higher and drier ground.

It is to one of the heaths that I often return. In the summer I can walk among the purple moor grass, the sedges and the reeds, and feel that time is standing still. In spite of its close association with man, the area has a strange feeling of distance from the world of humans. There is a hint of the primeval. The feeling of isolation is enhanced by the encircling *carr*, a belt of rough woodland, birch, alder or willow, with which many of the heaths are surrounded and which constantly threatens to encroach. In places the old pasture is already overtaken by dense patches of scrub birch and bog myrtle.

On a sunny day the atmosphere within the magic circle of birch and alder is hotly oppressive and yet brimming with pent-up energy. From a thicket I can hear the 'ticker' of a grasshopper warbler. There are insects everywhere, and the air seems to vibrate with the activities of so many thousands of living creatures. Butterflies, meadow browns, flutter languidly among the vegetation. Dragonflies patrol their territories in predatory fashion, the click of their wings sounding quite distinctly. Towards evening a heron flies over after a day spent fishing in the rhines. A barn owl takes flight at my approach and on the drove leading from the heath back to the road a pair of hares start up.

The Somerset Levels – where Man and Nature have worked side by side. Like many other wetlands in Britain, this area is in need of protection.

23

It is a place I love at any and every season. In spring to the cry of the waders, in a rolling autumn mist or the frosts of winter, I go there in the happy certainty of being both delighted and absorbed. I can rest content, too, in the knowledge that the heath and its wildlife are safe for the future, since it is a nature reserve. One can easily forget in the enjoyment of such places that their continued existence is only made possible by the efforts of many people. My special heath is among nearly thirty reserves in the care of the local Nature Conservation Trust, and these are but a fraction of the total number of reserves managed by all the Nature Conservation Trusts throughout Britain.

The Trusts were founded independently over a period of several years, and there are now forty-two of them covering the whole of Britain. The first, Norfolk, was founded in 1920 – but the majority have been formed since the last war, mostly in response to the growing threat to the environment in the 1960s. I regard the local Trusts as the most important factor in the voluntary conservation movement in Britain. This is not to denigrate in any way the activities of other conservation organisations, it is simply to acknowledge the predominant role which the Trusts play in protecting wildlife. All are part of the same trend towards increasing awareness of the vulnerability of our natural heritage and a desire to ensure its survival for future generations to cherish and enjoy.

The Trusts came into being because like-minded people – professional scientists, amateur naturalists and those who are simply lovers of the countryside – joined forces to do something practical to conserve the natural life of their localities. Despite having been founded in a somewhat haphazard manner, the Trusts are markedly similar in their aims and in the ways in which they achieve greater public awareness of, and protection for, the wild plants and animals of the countryside.

One of the great strengths of the Trusts is their local emphasis. Their members have the knowledge which is essential if the right decisions are to be made on local conservation issues. A local organisation, however, if it is to be effective, needs a national platform. To achieve this the Nature Conservation Trusts are affiliated to a central organisation based in Lincolnshire, the Society for the Promotion of Nature Conservation. Membership of this association gives the Trusts many advantages without the need to surrender their autonomy.

The Society for the Promotion of Nature Conservation, or the SPNC as it is known, was founded in 1912 and, led by the Hon. Charles Rothschild, pioneered nature conservation in Britain. It prepared the first lists of areas of importance as wildlife habitats and was also largely instrumental in laying the foundations of government action in conservation, including the creation of the

Nature Conservancy (now the Nature Conservancy Council). The Society's role as the national association of the Nature Conservation Trusts really began in 1958, however, when the formation of Trusts, which until then had been a trickle, became a spate. The SPNC now has a full and active part to play in the development of the Trusts, and this wider objective was officially recognised in 1976 when a new Royal Charter was granted.

The Trusts and the SPNC have always put the conservation of habitat before the preservation of particular species, in the belief that if a habitat is properly managed, the plants and animals which depend on it will thrive. The most obvious way to achieve this is by the establishment of nature reserves. Some people seem to be under the impression that 'nature reserves' and 'nature conservation' are synonymous – certainly the acquisition of reserves is fundamental to conservation, but there is very much more than this to the work of the Trusts.

Natural history and the conservation of nature have suffered in the past from an 'elitist' image, as the prerogative of a privileged few. Now, happily, nature conservation is recognised as being the concern of us all. The people who order the day-by-day running of the Trusts and the SPNC and carry out the many and varied projects are alive to the needs of the modern world, but they are convinced of the vital need to temper the progress of our own species with a well-informed and caring attitude to the needs of wildlife, wild places and the relationship between these and the environment as a whole. Conservationists, whether professional or amateur, are individuals who really care about what is happening to the world which we all share, and they are prepared to get their boots muddy in the cause.

Fortunate is the person whose work he or she not only enjoys but also considers to be worth while. I had that privilege (and, indeed, still do in my present work with the World Wildlife Fund) during the five years in which I was employed by the Somerset Trust for Nature Conservation. I must admit, however, that at the start of my career I knew very little about practical nature conservation and even less about the working of a Nature Conservation Trust. Somerset is a county which I know well and love deeply. It was a bonus that my opportunity to work in conservation coincided with a return to what I regarded as my native county, if not by birth then by adoption. The wetlands of the Somerset Levels where I now live have many conservation problems which are unique to the area, but they have also been described as a classic example of the conflict, real and potential, between wildlife and agriculture. They illustrate well the varied aspects of the work of any of the Nature Conservation Trusts up and down the country.

The present face of the Somerset Levels is the result of man's activities since the eighteenth century and his development of more efficient methods of flood prevention and control. The waters of the Bristol Channel and of the many rivers which drain into the area could well submerge many parts of the Levels permanently. The sea walls and the system of gates, sluices and pumping stations ensure that this does not happen. The numerous ditches, rhines and larger channels, known as drains, are all part of this system and of the wildlife habitat which it has created.

Traditionally the Levels are permanent pasture, grazed in summer but waterlogged in winter. In the past farming co-existed harmoniously with wildlife, but modern pressures have forced farmers to reconsider their methods. New drainage schemes, although expensive, enable land to be used for more months in the year. Old grassland, a habitat rich in plant and animal life, is ploughed and replaced with cereal or root crops, thus destroying a wealth of wildlife. Change is slow to come on the Levels but the trends are there, as they are everywhere.

Apart from the richness of its plant life and the animal and bird populations which this supports, the Levels are used for overwintering by many species of wildfowl and waders. One of the pleasures of the Levels in winter is the sight of flocks of teal, pintail and widgeon. The selection of the best wildlife habitats as nature reserves is the obvious, although not the only, solution to the conflict of interests between the human and non-human users of our landscape.

What exactly is a nature reserve? To many people the words conjure up an image of securely padlocked gates and signs which say 'No Admittance'. To others the words mean beautiful landscapes where visitors are welcome to walk and picnic and where they can discover more about the countryside. Both these ideas are partly true. Some wildlife habitats are so fragile that too many visitors would destroy the very thing they are intending to protect. Soil erosion, for example, and the disruption of delicately balanced communities of plants from the pressure of many pairs of feet, can cause permanent damage to areas of great natural significance. In such places it is only sensible to limit access to those who wish to make specialised studies. Similarly other reserves may be closed at certain times of the year when disturbance to the natural balance would be most severe, such as during the breeding season.

There are, however, many habitats which are sufficiently robust to be able to absorb the attentions of numbers of visitors without sustaining undue damage. If a Nature Conservation Trust, or any other conservation body with land under its care, has enough manpower to carry out the necessary maintenance work and provide wardens, it is usually only too willing for the public to visit and enjoy and learn from these places. Where open access is not possible there are often locally publicised open days and guided walks of many reserves. I have listed a few of the places where the public is welcome.

It is, I suspect, a widely held belief that once a nature reserve has been so designated it can be left to take care of itself. This is seldom the case. Our countryside is largely man-made; since prehistoric times we have been changing and moulding the face of Britain through our agricultural methods and through industrial development. Man's activities have resulted in a patchwork of different habitats which in turn support varying species of plant and animal life. In order to maintain the richness and diversity of our wildlife each habitat needs careful and scientific attention. Some techniques now used in the management of nature reserves are rarely seen elsewhere. The coppicing of woodland, for example, which in former times had commercial importance, would have vanished in many places were it not for its value in increasing the diversity of habitat.

This process of maintaining or improving the natural environment is a crucial aspect of the Trusts' policy of establishing nature reserves. The management programme recommended by a Trust's Conservation Officer and panel of expert naturalists is usually carried out by its own members, but in addition nature reserves benefit greatly from the work done by members of the British Trust for Conservation Volunteers. This is another voluntary organisation with many local branches whose members spend their free time carrying out an immense variety of practical conservation tasks. There are so many countryside organisations, both voluntary ones, such as the Trusts, and statutory ones such as the Nature Conservancy Council, that there is often confusion among members of the public as to who does what. I still find some of the demarcations confusing so I have compiled a brief list which I hope will clarify some of the more common misunderstandings.

As I have indicated, the Nature Conservation Trusts are not the only organisations which acquire and manage nature reserves. Other bodies and some private landowners are very active in this field. The Royal Society for the Protection of Birds manages some ninety nature reserves, generally quite large ones and selected primarily for their ornithological importance. The Society does an immense amount of work to protect birds and has had some spectacular successes. It follows, too, that if a habitat is protected for its bird population it is also protected for the other wildlife which depends on it.

In addition to its advisory role to government, the Nature Conservancy Council is empowered to set up National Nature Reserves, and it now manages some 140 of these throughout the country. It also carries out much valuable work in identifying Sites of Special Scientific Interest, known unromantically as SSSIs. These are graded according to their importance, and it is interesting to note that nearly half the total area of nature reserves managed by the Nature Conservation Trusts is classified by the Nature Conservancy Council as Grade I.

Relations between the Nature Conservancy Council and the Trusts are excellent and their staff often work in close liaison. It is surely encouraging that a statutory body should recognise the tremendous contribution to conservation made by the voluntary organisations.

The Nature Conservation Trusts manage over 1200 reserves, large and small, ranging in importance from national to purely local interest. The Trusts' policy is to give certain sites priority for acquisition, for where money and manpower are at a premium it is essential that these resources are not squandered on sites of little natural value. The SPNC with its nationwide outlook can be of great help in assessing the relative merits of different sites.

In this respect liaison between the Trusts and other bodies is also important. The Somerset Trust for Nature Conservation and the Royal Society for the Protection of Birds, for example, have established a joint policy for their conservation activities on the Somerset Levels which will avoid duplication of effort and subsequent waste of resources. One step in the implementation of this policy is the purchase by the Trust, with the help of the World Wildlife Fund, of a small part of Tealham Moor, a wetland site which is important both botanically and ornithologically.

A number of nature reserves contain rarities and information on these is not, of course, made public. There is sometimes criticism of money being spent on the conservation of a particular species which many people feel would be better spent on the protection of the greatest number of species. Mention of rarities can so easily cloud the issue, for the point is that, if a particular rarity is protected on a reserve, all the other species associated with that habitat are also protected; the rarity, be it plant or animal, serves to stimulate interest in, and financial support for, the habitat as a whole. A Nature Conservation Trust in Wales has a five-acre reserve specifically for the spotted rock-rose, a vulnerable species, but that same site also supports many other plants such as spring squill, allseed and bird's-foot. Small reserves of this kind need special care as they are less able to withstand the pressure of outside influences or the natural fluctuations in the delicate balance of plant and animal communities.

At the other end of the spectrum are the large reserves. Loch of the Lowes, to take just one example, is an area of 242 acres containing mixed woodland and fresh water – two rich wildlife habitats. Owned and managed by the Scottish Wildlife Trust, the loch with its fringing woodland provides endless opportunities for study and research. But for those who wish simply to enjoy wildlife there is a vast wealth of species to observe: wildfowl and waders abound, as do many species of woodland bird; roe and fallow deer can be seen on or near the reserve; and birds of prey occur regularly.

Nature reserves, large and small, act as 'reservoirs' of natural resources, where the impact of man's activities and the ecological consequences of this

Loch of the Lowes, a nature reserve of nearly 250 acres owned by the Scottish Wildlife Trust and open to the public in spring and summer.

can be reduced to the minimum. They are havens for wildlife away from the pressures of the outside world. With a choice of over 1200 reserves in the care of the Nature Conservation Trusts it is impossible to give more than a glimpse of the immense richness and diversity of wildlife and countryside encompassed by their activities. But reserves are not the only places where wildlife flourishes; our total acreage of nature reserves in this country represents such a small proportion of the land surface that there would be no long-term prospects for wildlife if it were confined solely to reserves.

Land is needed for many essential purposes – for food production; industry; forestry; roads; buildings; sport and recreation. All are legitimate and necessary uses of our land resources but inevitably they conflict with wildlife to a certain extent. The Nature Conservation Trusts, and conservationists generally, try to mitigate this conflict as far as possible by a spirit of co-operation.

Farmers have under their control over three-quarters of the land in Britain and their goodwill is essential for the lasting protection of most wildlife habitats. The Trusts, in collaboration with the other bodies concerned with the countryside, have promoted county farming and wildlife advisory groups. Farmers and members of the agricultural advisory service have joined these local groups, and they help landowners with advice on hedgerows, tree planting, ponds and ditches, and how to improve wildlife on their land generally, without affecting the prosperity and good management of their farms. In two counties they have gone a stage further and employ full-time wildlife advisers.

This advisory role which the local Trusts play is largely unnoticed by the public but it is an increasingly important aspect of their work. Not only do they advise the owners or tenants of private land but they are also able to provide information for the planning departments of local authorities, water authorities and other statutory bodies. Decisions which affect wildlife can then be taken with a fuller understanding of the possible implications. Some local authorities have one or more Local Nature Reserves in their care and the Trusts give much technical advice and practical help with the management of these. Good liaison is also maintained with the Forestry Commission and independent forestry firms and with those concerned with the sporting and recreational uses of the countryside.

'Help a Toad across the Road' was the slogan of a campaign by the Herefordshire and Radnorshire Nature Trust to save one of Britain's largest toad colonies from decimation beneath the wheels of cars and lorries. The seasonal migration of the toads to their spawning grounds necessitates the crossing of a busy road. The toadlift first started in 1971, and every year a rota of volunteers from the Trust transports the toads in buckets across the road. Now Powys County Council has erected warning signs for motorists. As a result the road is safer – squashed toads create a very slippery surface – and the danger to the toad colony has been reduced. This is only a small example of co-operation between a Trust and a local authority, but it is of direct conservation value and does much to stimulate interest in conservation locally.

Official roadsigns reduce accidents to motorists as well as to toads.

Woods Mill at Henfield, Sussex. This eighteenth-century water mill contains an exhibition on wildlife and conservation, and is the centre of a small reserve and nature trail.

The conservation of wildlife has no long-term future unless enough people recognise the need for it and really want it. Children especially are encouraged to take an active interest through Watch, the national junior branch of the Trusts, and the field centres and other facilities available to schools. As part of their regular programmes the Trusts organise talks, film shows and field meetings for their members and the public. Many nature trails have been devised by the Trusts, often in co-operation with other organisations, to give people a greater opportunity to observe and understand wildlife.

Of growing importance is the setting up of information or interpretation centres on sites which are suitable for public access. Many Trusts have taken advantage of financial grants to provide a real service to the public in this respect. The Woods Mill headquarters of the Sussex Trust for Nature Conservation, for example, has nature trails through its fifteen acres of woodland and the eighteenth-century water mill itself contains an exhibition on the natural history of Sussex. The Lancashire Naturalists' Trust has pioneered a project for interpreting in detail a number of interesting sites and this has included the production of several publications. Much of the interpretation is for those with specific interests or needs: the Glasson Dock and Lune Estuary Trail, for example, was devised for anglers and boatmen, and Samlesbury Hall Nature Trail for the benefit of the disabled and elderly.

Many of the Trusts employ full-time staff. Some have permanent head-quarters and need not only Conservation Officers and Reserve Wardens but personnel to deal with the educational, promotional and administrative aspects of an expanding organisation. All of this requires money. Funds for major projects – the purchase of nature reserves or of vital tools and equipment for reserve management – may come from sources outside the Trusts. The World Wildlife Fund, for instance, is an international organisation which raises funds for conservation world-wide. It is a major source of financial help to the Trusts, as part of its acknowledged role in Britain is support for the existing network of conservation organisations, particularly in land acquisition and education. The effectiveness of the Trusts' work has been greatly enhanced by the financial support of the Nature Conservancy Council for reserve management projects. Unfortunately many factors, including government policy on public spending, severely affect the Nature Conservancy Council's capacity, though not its willingness, to assist the voluntary sector.

In spite of these contributions, expenditure by the Trusts on major projects represents an enormous commitment of their own resources. None of the Trusts could continue to operate effectively without the support, both financial and otherwise, of their many thousands of members. Volunteers created the Trusts and it is their time and expertise, unstintingly given, which enable the Trusts to expand and develop. Every skill or talent, from cake-baking to tree-felling, from typing to photography, can be used. All who care about the wild-life of this country have something to offer, just as the Trusts have a great deal to offer us in return. After all, in its broadest sense conservation is about people and for people.

We need wildlife and wild places not just for the physical well-being of our environment but for the simple enjoyment, emotional satisfaction and refresh-ment of spirit which we find in them. Not all of us are fortunate enough to live in the country; in fact for social, cultural and economic reasons the vast majority live in towns and cities – some of course may prefer to do so. But there cannot be many of us who do not relish the opportunity of visiting the countryside, for delight in its beauty, for quiet contemplation of the wild plants and animals, or simply for relaxation. We take pleasure in the know-ledge that this, our natural heritage, will survive for future generations. As Gerard Manley Hopkins wrote:

> *What would the world be, once bereft*
> *Of wet and wildness? Let them be left,*
> *O let them be left, wildness and wet;*
> *Long live the weeds and the wilderness yet.*

Gazetteer of
Nature Reserves
Open to the Public

The Nature Conservation Trusts have under their control some 1200 nature reserves. These are either owned or leased by the Trusts or managed by agreement with the owners. In addition the Trusts also act in an advisory capacity to local authorities and other landowners.

In certain cases members of Trusts are entitled to visit nature reserves not open to the public, and many Trusts will issue permits on a temporary basis to non-members. It is often possible for special arrangements to be made for school parties and educational visits by adults. Many reserves which are normally closed have special Open Days which are publicised locally. Details of membership and access to reserves can be obtained from individual Trusts.

The sites I have selected are those in which there is close involvement by the local Trust in one way or another and which are accessible in whole or in part to the general public. They vary both in size and in the types of wildlife which predominate, but they are representative of the vast amount of work carried out by the Nature Conservation Trusts.

In order to protect the habitat and its wildlife most Trusts have regulations or codes of conduct which visitors are expected to observe. For example, dogs are not normally allowed in nature reserves. Times of opening and the charging of admission or car park fees may be subject to alteration.

In this limited selection of nature reserves and trails I have tried to find something to suit all tastes and I hope you enjoy visiting the sites as much as I enjoyed choosing them.

To enable you to see at a glance what is of particular interest on each site, there is a key indicating the type of wildlife or habitat which is of special importance or is predominant. Lack of a symbol does not mean, however, that a site is necessarily devoid of that category of natural history; some of the sites which are especially rich in wildlife and very diverse are of general rather than specialised interest.

Nature Reserves

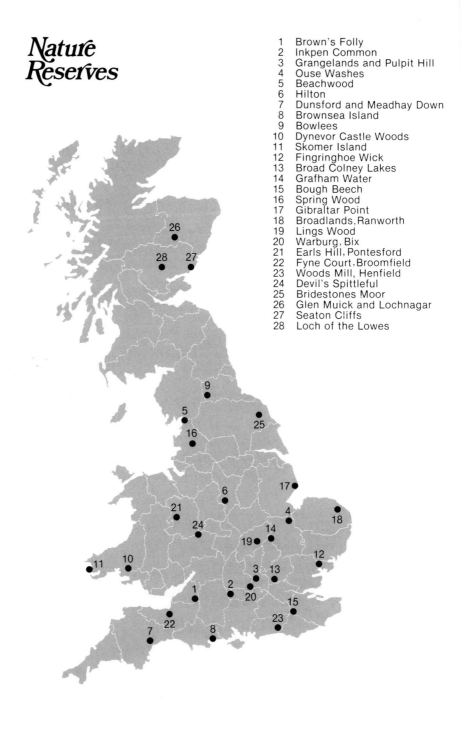

1   Brown's Folly
2   Inkpen Common
3   Grangelands and Pulpit Hill
4   Ouse Washes
5   Beachwood
6   Hilton
7   Dunsford and Meadhay Down
8   Brownsea Island
9   Bowlees
10 Dynevor Castle Woods
11 Skomer Island
12 Fingringhoe Wick
13 Broad Colney Lakes
14 Grafham Water
15 Bough Beech
16 Spring Wood
17 Gibraltar Point
18 Broadlands, Ranworth
19 Lings Wood
20 Warburg, Bix
21 Earls Hill, Pontesford
22 Fyne Court, Broomfield
23 Woods Mill, Henfield
24 Devil's Spittleful
25 Bridestones Moor
26 Glen Muick and Lochnagar
27 Seaton Cliffs
28 Loch of the Lowes

Key to symbols

 Botanical  Ornithological  Woodland

 Entomological  Water  Visitor Centre

Note: The Information or Interpretative Centres run by many of the Nature Conservation Trusts often also act as headquarters for the Trust concerned. In many cases they contain other facilities such as a shop for the sale of literature and gifts.

England and Wales

Avon

Brown's Folly Nature Reserve 31 acres of woodland and downland on the eastern outskirts of Bath. Brown's Folly was purchased as a nature reserve in 1971 by the Somerset Trust for Nature Conservation and is now managed by the Avon Wildlife Trust. There is a nature trail. The reserve is reached from the A4 Bath to Chippenham road.

Berkshire

Inkpen Common 26 acres of heathland leased by the Berkshire, Buckinghamshire and Oxfordshire Naturalists' Trust. Situated at Inkpen, south-east of Hungerford, it lies between the high chalk downs on the Hampshire border and the Kennet Valley.

Buckinghamshire

Grangelands and Pulpit Hill 50 acres of chalk downland, scrub and beech-wood, managed by the Berkshire, Buckinghamshire and Oxfordshire Naturalists' Trust by agreement with the owners. Access on foot is via the bridleway from the top of Longdown Hill towards the Upper Ick-nield Way or via the bridleway from Great Kimble to Longdown Hill.

Cambridgeshire

Bird Hides on the Ouse Washes Hides provided by both the Cambridge-shire and Isle of Ely Naturalists' Trust and the RSPB. The car park is at Welches Dam near Manea off the A142, where there is also a Visitor Centre containing an exhibition on the history and natural history of the fens. The hides are open to the public during daylight hours. A useful booklet on the Ouse Washes is available.

Cumbria

Beachwood 1–2 acres of woodland and meadow on the shore of the Kent estuary at Arnside, owned by Arnside Parish Council and managed by Cumbria Naturalists' Trust. The habitat is typical of the Arnside district. Access is on foot, 500 yards south-west along the shore from Arnside promenade.

Derbyshire

Hilton Gravel Pits 74 acres of flooded pits, scrub and woodland owned by Derbyshire Naturalists' Trust. Hilton is situated 7 miles west of Derby.

Devonshire

Dunsford and Meadhay Down 140 acres of woodland with clearings, rich in wildlife, along the Teign valley. The reserve is leased by the Devon Trust for Nature Conservation from the National Trust and Fulford Estates. It is situated 9 miles west of Exeter and access is from the B3212 Exeter to Moretonhampstead road, or from the Dunsford to Drewsteignton road. There is an illustrated information board at the Steps Bridge end of the reserve. A booklet is available.

Dorset

Brownsea Island The island is owned by the National Trust and is open to the public from Easter to September. It contains a great diversity of wildlife, besides being renowned for its peacocks. There is a frequent boat service from Poole and Sandbanks, and a landing fee is charged. The nature reserve on the island is managed by Dorset Naturalists' Trust. The Trust organises conducted tours of the reserve daily at 2.30 p.m. during the season. There is a small charge for the tour.

Durham

Bowlees Visitor Centre and Gibson's Cave Nature Trail The Visitor Centre is leased by the Durham County Conservation Trust and contains a display on the history and natural history of the area. It is open daily from Easter to October, between 10.00 a.m. and 5.00 p.m. There is a small admission charge. Bowlees is approximately 4 miles from Middleton and $\frac{3}{4}$ mile beyond Newbiggin. Access is by footpath from the Durham County Council car park and picnic site. A leaflet is available for the nature trail.

Dyfed

Dynevor Castle Woods 60 acres of woodland, with oak predominating but smaller amounts of ash, sycamore, wild cherry and beech, owned by West Wales Naturalists' Trust. The woodland is situated on the outskirts of Llandeilo and a footpath leads into the reserve from Llandeilo Bridge. A leaflet is available.

Skomer Island The island is a National Nature Reserve of 720 acres and is situated off the coast of Dyfed to the south-west. The reserve is managed by West Wales Naturalists' Trust and is famous for seabirds and seals. The island is open daily from Easter to September, except on Mondays (excluding Bank Holiday Mondays). There is a boat service from Martinshaven, weather permitting. A landing fee is charged.

Essex

Fingringhoe Wick Interpretative Centre and Nature Trail 125 acres of disused gravel workings and adjacent saltings owned by Essex Naturalists' Trust. Non-members may visit the Centre and walk some of the nature trails between 9.00 a.m. and 4.30 p.m., Tuesdays to Saturdays (except on the day after a Bank Holiday). Booklets are available. There is no admission charge, but non-members are invited to make a small donation. The reserve is situated off the B1025 Colchester to Mersea Island road.

Hertfordshire

Broad Colney Lakes 27 acres owned by the Hertfordshire and Middlesex Trust for Nature Conservation, consisting of a stretch of the river Colne with associated flooded gravel pits and their surrounding woodland and grassland. The reserve is open daily during daylight hours and there is a car park on the west side adjoining Shenley Lane. The reserve is situated at London Colney south of the A405.

Huntingdonshire

Bird Hide at Grafham Water A reserve of 370 acres at the western end of Grafham Water Reservoir, managed by the Bedfordshire and Huntingdonshire Naturalists' Trust by agreement with the Anglian Water Authority. Access to the reserve is restricted but the public are welcome to use the bird hide for a small charge. The hide, which overlooks a bird sanctuary, is open on Sundays only from September to February, 9.30 a.m. to 5.30 p.m. or dusk (whichever is earlier). The hide should be approached from Mander car park, West Perry, where the Warden is on duty. Grafham Water is situated a short way from the A1 at Buckden.

Kent

Bough Beech Interpretative Centre 45 acres at the north end of Bough Beech Reservoir, leased as a nature reserve by the Kent Trust for Nature Conservation. The Interpretative Centre is a converted oasthouse and contains an exhibition covering all aspects of the history, natural history and previous land-use of the reservoir. There is a part-time Warden and the Centre is open to the public most weekends. A useful booklet is available and a nature trail is in preparation.

Lancashire

Spring Wood An area of mixed woodland with picnic sites and car park, owned by Lancashire County Council and managed with advice from Lancashire Naturalists' Trust. The Trust has prepared an excellent guide interpreting the ecological features of the wood. Spring Wood is situated off the A59 (Burnley turn-off).

Lincolnshire

Gibraltar Point A local authority Local Nature Reserve managed by the Lincolnshire and South Humberside Trust for Nature Conservation and consisting of 1500 acres of sand dunes, salt marshes, seashore, dune slacks and freshwater habitats. It is of great scientific importance, but for the general visitor there is a Centre containing displays on the history and development of the area and on the wildlife. There is also a bird hide. A network of paths cross the reserve, for which a booklet is available. The Visitor Centre and walks are open at weekends from November to Easter, Saturdays 2.00 p.m. to 5.00 p.m. and Sundays 10.00 a.m. to 1.00 p.m. and 2.00 p.m. to 5.00 p.m. and daily from Easter to October, 10.00 a.m. to 5.00 p.m. The reserve extends from the southern end of Skegness approximately 3 miles to the entrance of the Wash.

Norfolk

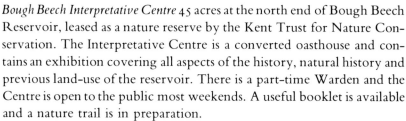

Broadlands Conservation Centre, Ranworth This unspoilt Broad is owned by Norfolk Naturalists' Trust. The Centre, a thatched building floating on pontoons, contains an exhibition on the history and natural history of the Broads. It is open daily (except Mondays) from April to October, 10.00 a.m. to 5.00 p.m. and on Saturdays 2.00 p.m. to 5.00 p.m. Wednesday afternoons are reserved for party bookings. There is a small admission charge. Cars must be left in the car park opposite the public staithe. The nature trail leading to the Centre starts about 400 yards from the car park, nearly opposite Ranworth Village Hall. Ranworth is situated 9 miles from Norwich via the B1140 and 12 miles from Great Yarmouth via Acle.

Northamptonshire

Lings Wood Countryside Interpretative Centre 15 acres of mixed woodland with conifer plantations, leased by Northamptonshire Naturalists' Trust. Lings House in the middle of the woodland contains an Information Centre and exhibition rooms. There is a nature trail and a booklet is available. The Centre is open from Mondays to Fridays, 9.00 a.m. to 5.00 p.m., and evenings or weekends by arrangement. The reserve is situated between Lings and Blackthorn housing estates on the A45 Northampton to Wellingborough road, approximately 3¾ miles north-east of Northampton.

Oxfordshire

Warburg Reserve, Bix 247 acres of beech and mixed woodland, scrub and grassland, owned by the Berkshire, Buckinghamshire and Oxfordshire Naturalists' Trust. The reserve is an outstanding botanical site and contains a nature trail and Information Centre. There is a residential Warden and appointments can be made in advance. A useful leaflet is available. The reserve car park is reached via the roads leading to Bix Bottom from the A423 at Bix or from the B480 at Middle Assendon.

Shropshire

Earls Hill Nature Trail, Pontesford 100 acres of grassland, woodland, cliff and scree, owned by the Shropshire Conservation Trust. The hill trail is arduous but very varied and a booklet is available. Cars should be left in Pontesford and the trail approached on foot. The timber-framed barn at Earls Hill Farm has been restored by the Trust as a Conservation Centre. It is open on Saturday and Sunday afternoons in the summer or by special arrangement for parties. The reserve is situated ½ mile from the A488 Shrewsbury to Bishops Castle road, 7 miles south-west of Shrewsbury.

Somerset

Fyne Court Visitor Centre, Broomfield 24 acres of woodland walks with ponds and streams, leased by the Somerset Trust for Nature Conservation from the National Trust. There is a picnic area and car park. The Interpretation Centre contains an exhibition on natural history and conservation. It is open daily between 9.00 a.m. and 6.00 p.m. Leaflets and booklets are available. Broomfield is situated on the Quantock Hills, 6 miles north of Taunton and 8 miles west of Bridgwater.

Sussex

Woods Mill, Henfield 15 acres of woodland, marsh, streams and lake with nature trails and an eighteenth-century water mill, owned by the Sussex Trust for Nature Conservation. The mill contains an exhibition on wildlife and conservation. Booklets are available for the nature trail. Woods Mill is open from May to September on Sundays and Bank Holidays, 11.00 a.m. to 6.00 p.m., and on Tuesdays, Wednesdays, Thursdays and Saturdays, 2.00 p.m. to 6.00 p.m. There is a small admission charge. It is situated at the junction of the A2037 and Horn Lane leading to Woodmancote.

Worcestershire

Devil's Spittleful and Rifle Range 150 acres of sandy heathland, birch woodland and grassland, managed by the Worcestershire Trust for Nature Conservation by agreement with the owners. A number of public footpaths cross the area. The rocky knoll known as the Devil's Spittleful is of considerable geological interest. The reserve is situated off the A456 between Bewdley and Kidderminster and access is along the track beside the entrance to West Midland Safari Park.

Yorkshire

Bridestones Moor Woodland and open moor with streams, owned by the National Trust and managed jointly with Yorkshire Naturalists' Trust. A nature walk has been set out in this typical area of the North York Moors and a leaflet is available. The Bridestones themselves are of great geological interest. The reserve is situated in the North York Moors National Park on the edge of Dalby Forest, 1 mile east of the A169.

Scotland

Aberdeenshire

Glen Muick and Lochnagar Wildlife Reserve 6350 acres of moorland and mountain habitats, managed for wildlife by the Scottish Wildlife Trust by agreement with Balmoral Estates. The Visitor Centre contains an exhibition on red deer and information about the surrounding area. There are a number of pleasant walks but some are suitable for advanced walkers only. It is open daily during the summer months.

Angus

Seaton Cliffs 26 acres of red sandstone cliffs owned by the Scottish Wildlife Trust. The Arbroath Cliffs nature trail, which starts at the north end of the promenade in Arbroath, is set partly in the reserve. An excellent booklet is available.

Perthshire

Loch of the Lowes Visitor Centre 242 acres of loch with its fringing woodland, owned by the Scottish Wildlife Trust. The Centre contains an exhibition about the wildlife of the area which includes red deer, and there is a bird hide. Booklets and leaflets are available. It is open daily in April, May and September, 10.00 a.m. to 7.00 p.m., and in June, July and August, 10.00 a.m. to 8.30 p.m. The reserve is situated 2 miles east of Dunkeld off the A923 Blairgowrie road.

Further details about these and other sites managed by the Nature Conservation Trusts can be obtained from the individual Trusts. The addresses of all 42 Trusts in Britain are listed in the Appendix on page 198.

Eric Hosking's Special Reserve

ANGELA RIPPON

'Eric who?' I asked. 'Eric Hosking,' said the voice of the *In the Country* producer on the other end of the telephone. 'He's a bird photographer and we want you to sit with him in a hide on the Dee Estuary taking photographs for three hours as part of a film we're making about his work.'

Now sitting in a cramped and draughty canvas box three feet square on the bare, bleak mudflats opposite Liverpool on a Sunday in October is not my idea of the perfect way to spend a precious free weekend. Especially with someone I'd never heard of! Frankly I wasn't keen.

But when the research material dropped through my letterbox two days later, and I tipped the contents of the large buff envelope out on to the study floor, I suddenly realised just *who* it was that I was being asked to work with.

There, all around me, were pictures of owls, birds of prey, seabirds, garden birds; birds of every shape, size and hue that filled the calendars and books which had been the foundations of my interest in wildlife. I may not have known the photographer's name, but his photographs were like old friends.

Eric Hosking is quite rightly accepted as one of the greatest wildlife photographers of the age – though his work is far better known to the world at large than either his face or his name. And it's typical of the man that he believes that's just as it should be. But then anyone who can take a fuzzy, badly exposed shot of a song thrush's nest with a five-shilling box Brownie at the age of seven, and know from that moment on that birds and cameras were to be as important in his life as food and drink, has to be someone with a very special attitude to his work. Eric has always been far more concerned with perfecting his art than promoting his name, and it wasn't really until he reached his seventieth birthday in 1979, when the BBC and photographic companies began to acknowledge his contribution to wildlife photography, that he became as widely known and recognisable as his photographs.

42

And so here was I being offered the chance of a lifetime, to practise my own hobby of photography under the guiding hand of one of the greatest experts in the world. Suddenly, spending an autumnal Sunday morning on the mudflats of the Dee wasn't such a bad proposition after all.

The Dee Estuary sits in the cleft of a right-angle on the west coast of Britain, with Liverpool on one side and Wales on the other. When the tide is in, there's nothing to be seen but a vast expanse of water stretching out to the Irish sea. But when the tide recedes it exposes more than 65 square miles of wave-rippled mud, a rich feeding ground for the flocks of migrant and native seabirds who wing across that section of coast throughout the year. As the tide returns it gradually pushes the birds further and further inland, until eventually they are herded like sheep on to the banks of the river and the small outcrops and islands dotted along its course.

Little Eye and Hilbre Island are two of the landfalls made famous by Eric's photographs. As 6 October was to produce the highest tide of the year, it would also, we hoped, produce the most spectacular gathering of seabirds.

I arrived on Little Eye at 10.00 a.m. on foot, having left our film crew Land Rover stuck in the black soggy mud with the tide on the turn, and a full-scale rescue operation in force. I settled myself on a rock on the island, and waited. Not for the birds – it would be another three hours or more before they came in any numbers – but for the bird man, Eric Hosking.

When he arrived, my impression was of a small man with tiny feet, looking at least ten years short of his seventy and radiating enough energy to service a power station. I adored him on sight. Taking a fatherly grip on my elbow he walked me across to his own Land Rover, drove me the mile and a half over rocks and rivulets to Hilbre Island, and invited me into the house which has been the base for him and his fellow enthusiasts for almost fifty years. And all the time he talked with passion and drive about birds: watching them, photographing them, studying them – loving them.

There are no half measures with Eric. Once he senses that you have an interest in what is his passion he absorbs you totally into his winged world. Within an hour the film crew had been winched out of the mud by the sailing school tractor, in which time Eric and I had gossiped and giggled our way through his life, my life, people we admired, things we disliked, and the sort of topics we would discuss once we started filming.

As soon as the cameras began rolling, it became clear that even though personal fame had come late in life to Eric Hosking, he was going to enjoy every minute of it.

He was a natural, a real pro. Some people, when faced with the paraphernalia of a camera, sound recordist, director and production secretary will dry up, go flat, or be so embarrassed and unnatural that they can hardly recognise themselves. Not Eric. He treated the prying eye and ear of the television crew with the natural, unaffected behaviour he expects from his own winged sitters. He stopped on cue, moved on cue, and said the right thing at the right time so that we were able to film most sequences without a single retake.

As the morning wore on, the tide advanced towards the shore and we all got ready for the long vigil inside the hide. Eric's son, David, had set up the hide and installed the equipment so that all Eric and I had to do was clip on the remote-controlled microphones and transmitters, then creep into the green sailcloth tent – and wait.

The hide was perched right on the edge of a shallow cliff overlooking Lion Rock, a small lump of local sandstone some ten feet long, which at high tide would be literally encrusted with Sanderling, Redshank and Knot, all chattering and elbowing for territory. Once settled they would roost silently, with beaks twisted at rest under wings until their dinner table was once again exposed by the receding tide.

The island was packed with bird-watchers – one of the results of encouraging people's interest in birds through the magic of Eric Hosking's photographs and lectures is that they too want to see for themselves, be on the spot, take their own photographs. It's a situation that Eric accepts with equanimity. If they come just to observe, appreciate and learn, he's delighted. What he cannot tolerate are those people who disturb or upset the birds' life-style, never letting them feed or rest just for the sake of a better picture. 'The birds must come first' is Eric's maxim – which is why we settled ourselves inside the hide at least an hour before they began gathering in any great numbers. That way we wouldn't suddenly startle or disturb them.

Eric had his camera anchored to a solid tripod, with the most enormous lens I've ever seen mounted on the front. With this lens a bird sitting almost a hundred yards away, looking no bigger than a thumbnail to the human eye, could be magnified to fill the frame as if it were perched right outside our peephole. My own camera was far more modest, with a shorter-range lens and I didn't have the advantage of a tripod. Lesson number one from Mr Hosking to Miss Rippon was: 'Get the camera mounted on something, otherwise you risk ruining your best pictures with camera shake.'

As we waited, the tide moved relentlessly forward and the birds began to wheel and gather overhead, settling ten, twenty, fifty at a time on the rock in front of our cameras until the air was filled with the screeching and calling of tens of thousands of them. We spoke in whispers, and moved slowly and cautiously. The scene outside was building up into something far too precious to lose through a careless noise or blunder.

We seemed by then to have been talking non-stop for hours. But you don't condense seventy action-packed years into a few glib sentences, and there was

Above: Angela Rippon sets off with Eric Hosking for a day of bird-watching and photography on Hilbre Island off the Wirral Peninsula. Note the sturdy tripod Eric is carrying.

Below: Angela and Eric snap their pictures at almost the same moment. Eric's photograph (inset) was taken with a long telephoto lens and clearly shows the group of Common Red-shank, Knot and Turnstone that were roosting some fifty yards in front of the hide.

still so much to hear about his life, and learn about his art. He recounted, for example, how in those early days of the 1930s he had humped tons of wildly impractical, cumbersome equipment all over the world just to catch a bird in flight, or nesting. He told me about his honeymoon spent in Scotland filming Golden Eagles; about the filing system he has for the 90,000 colour transparencies and the 250,000 black and white photographs he keeps in the study of his London home; about the satisfaction he derives from lecturing and the delight of helping to develop new equipment and techniques in wildlife photography. He told me too of the night a Tawny Owl snatched the sight of his left eye. 'It wasn't the owl's fault,' he says staunchly. 'I was photographing her nest, she was protecting her young. I don't attach any blame whatever to that Tawny Owl.' That happened in Wales in 1937. A lesser man might have been stopped in his tracks – but not Eric Hosking. As he says, 'You only need one eye to look through the viewfinder of a camera.' And we were busy doing just that.

On the end of my lens I found Redshank, Knot and a few stray Oyster-catchers, all perched so close that I felt I could reach out and smooth their wind-ruffled feathers. I clicked my way through three rolls of film, almost a hundred pictures, with Eric suggesting, coaxing and teaching. 'Try a different angle here, a change of exposure or speed there, try to follow flight,' and so on.

For three hours we worked away inside the hide, while outside at a distance the BBC crew filmed and recorded – eavesdropping and illustrating, without ever intruding, either on us or the birds.

At the end of the day I was invited to join Eric and the rest of the house party for a feast of French bread, a mug of steaming coffee, and what looked like a gallon of freshly caught shrimps smothered in black pepper. Around the walls of the main living room there were scores of photographs, all of them depicting the Hilbre house party guests: Prince Philip, Lord Alanbrooke, some of the most famous amateur and professional photographers and ornithologists – but *no* women. 'Ladies aren't usually invited,' I was told. 'We don't even let our wives join us here. This is strictly a bachelor reserve. But for Eric we're delighted to bend the rules and let you join us.'

Later we all trooped outside on to the small terrace overlooking the now empty Lion Rock for the traditional group photograph. There I was, the only woman guest ever allowed to invade the bachelor reserve of Hilbre Island. It was indeed an honour, but what I treasure most were those three hours in the hide taking pictures with the greatest bird photographer in the world.

The Brickmaker

BERNARD PRICE

Place names frequently provide clues to the past use of land. Obvious examples are 'Brick Field', 'Tile Lane' or 'Brick-kiln Farm', but places bearing these names today seldom show any trace of such previous activity.

Wherever suitable clay proved to be available, brickmaking seems to have followed and, in the majority of cases, was successfully combined with farming. In the sixteenth century brickyards were also established on large estates to build the great houses of the period, and this practice carried on until the eighteenth century. The demand for bricks continued to expand with the fast-growing population of Victorian times. Many nineteenth-century photographs show brick carts moving through towns, and visits to brickfields feature strongly in the contents of children's books at that time. After all, there is nothing so constructive as a good brick.

In later years, rich clay-bearing areas were taken over by the large companies and the Second World War rang the death knell for most of the small family brickfields that still remained. Owners either joined the armed services or turned entirely to farming, which was made a priority industry. Another factor that brought about closures at that time was that the commonly used updraught brick kilns contravened black-out regulations whenever they were fired, and only a handful of brickfields with downdraught kilns were able to continue. These were in due course also given the status of priority industries, making such products as drainpipes for the drainage of farms and military airfields. So it was that some family businesses have continued to thrive into the final quarter of the twentieth century.

In the valley of the Stour, in Suffolk, Peter Minter inherited from his father a farm and brickworks situated along a seam of London clay; it could hardly have been better placed. His father was a builder specialising in restoring Tudor houses who, frequently finding himself unable to obtain bricks of the decorative shape required to match old work, began to make 'specials' in his own brickyard. The family farmhouse itself carries examples of his skill.

Making the moulds for such bricks is a highly skilled craft requiring the making of individual wooden copings and plinths that are fitted into a wooden box mould. Each different shape requires a new mould and the task of the mould maker is to create an intaglio shape which will yield a cameo brick identical to those it supplements or replaces. When making the moulds the shrinkage of the clay during firing has to be taken into account. It is the production of such 'specials', frequently used in the restoration of some of the finest houses and palaces in England, that has given a small business of this kind the opportunity to flourish today.

Making the moulds for individual bricks is a highly skilled craft. Here Peter Minter works a wooden intaglio shape which will yield a cameo brick.

Suffolk is rich in the clay needed to make the bricks in which Peter Minter specialises. These bricks are made of clay dug from his own farm.

The basic brickmaking process has barely changed over the years. Clay is dug twice a year, in early summer and in autumn. Allowed to 'weather' before use, it is then churned in a pug mill to the required consistency. The maker takes in his hands a lump of clay of a size slightly larger than the mould, called a 'warp', and after dusting it with sand throws it into a sanded mould. Making the standard brick is a simple operation but the 'specials' take far more time, for the clay must be pushed firmly into the moulds to fill the decorative and functional mouldings. With the excess clay removed, the brick is then turned out on to a board and taken to be dried.

Standard bricks are dried in the open air beneath narrow roofed shelters known as 'hacks'. In midsummer they may be ready for the kiln in a week; at other times they may take six to eight weeks. The special bricks are oven dried; this takes ten to fourteen days, for if they were allowed to dry too quickly the bricks would crack.

The firing of the kiln may last four days. It is an expensive business with increasing fuel costs, but the result is brickwork of warmth and beauty that has delighted the eye for centuries. In the case of Peter Minter the future too seems assured, for his own children are interested in continuing the craft into the next generation.

Heavy Horse Power

JOE HENSON

Being a London boy and living within half an hour of the West End by tube, I was lucky to live near enough to a farm to cycle to work there on leaving school. I consider that I was even luckier that in the early 1950s the farm only had one tractor and was run almost entirely with horses. The boss was a kind man but a hard task master and I had to get to work by 5.00 a.m., either to help hand milk the cows or to prepare the horses for work. This, I was constantly reminded by the carter, was late compared with when he was a boy. However early I got to work I never managed to arrive before him.

My Dad, who was an actor, kept very different hours and during that part of my life we only met on my day off. He, too, was pleased about the type of farm on which I was apprenticed, but for a different reason. He realised that the 'all graft and no glamour' type of farming would kill or confirm my ambition to farm. The fact that it was confirmed is, I am sure, largely due to the beautiful and long-suffering cart horses with which I was privileged to learn. They never once took advantage of my clumsy ineptitude and, unlike the men on the farm, never even laughed. I remember their names to this day, Tom, Flower, Molly and the others. Although my career in farm management and then tenant farming has taken me by necessity into high-powered tractors, I still love and respect the working horse.

The history of the heavy horse dates back to the Middle Pleistocene period when there is archaeological evidence of a large, heavy, marsh-dwelling horse living in the Rhine Valley. It appears to have been a fairly localised type unlike the fast, light horses that grazed the plains in the rest of Europe and Asia, and was certainly the ancestor of today's heavy horses. The closest living survivor of this early type is the Ardennes breed of France, very similar to the Flemish horse which played an important part in the ancestry of our heavy horse breeds of today. The use of the 'Great Horse' as a war horse was prompted by the change-over from chain mail to plate armour in the fourteenth century; by the fifteenth century armour had become so weighty that the heavy war horse was a vital strategic weapon.

Presenting In the Country *brings Angela Rippon's world of TV into contact with two of her greatest loves – the countryside and horses.*

Angela Rippon at Phil Drabble's home in Staffordshire, where many kinds of wild and domestic creatures have the freedom of his woodland nature reserve.

For Phil Drabble, working dogs are an essential part of the country scene. Here he finds out more about foxhounds from Michael Farrin, huntsman for the renowned Quorn Kennels in Lincolnshire.

Bernard Price and Gordon Beningfield at Orford in Suffolk, waiting to cross by boat to the R.S.P.B. bird reserve on Havergate Island.

Angela Rippon introduces Phil Drabble to her own favourite countryside. Here on the edge of Dartmoor she and her husband Chris have renovated a traditional Devon cottage where they would like 'to live for the rest of our lives'.

A decree of Henry VIII, stating that all landowners must keep a stallion of over a certain height, did much to spread and establish the heavy horse in this country. The stallions were intended for battle because of their courage, but they also sired the mares on their owners' estates and left their mark to this day. With the passing of armour and the establishment of light cavalry, the heavy horse was demoted to the work of haulage on farms, roads and woodland, and finally replaced oxen as the power unit in agriculture towards the end of the nineteenth century.

Their reign on the farm was a short one. I know men alive today who worked with oxen in their youth and enjoyed the change to horses, but steam power soon arrived to take over the heaviest work. The coming of the internal combustion engine soon eliminated the heavy horse from road transport, but it hung on in farming and forestry until after the Second World War. Today we have no way of knowing how many remain on farms, as by 1960 their numbers had become so insignificant that they were removed from the annual agricultural census form. You can be sure that the number of farmers who, like Geoff Morton of Yorkshire, rely solely on the horse can be counted on your fingers.

Although many farm horses were crossbreds, the heavy horses of Britain can be divided into four distinct breeds. The best known and the most directly descended from the medieval Great Horse is the Shire. The biggest of our heavy horses, the stallions can attain a height of eighteen hands and weigh up to a ton.

When the spread of the Old English Great Horse reached over the border into Scotland another of today's breeds was evolved. Heavy stallions were mated with the smaller local horses containing Highland blood, which gave them hardiness and agility, and the Clydesdale was born. Like Shires, they have been supported by the breweries since falling out of wide-scale commercial use and are perhaps even more popular as dray horses due to their greater agility and speed.

Our rarest breed of heavy horse is certainly the Suffolk Punch. Like the Shire and the Clydesdale, its ancestry dates back to Flemish horses imported from Belgium but it had a mixture of many breeds in its early make-up, even, according to some authorities, the trotting horse. Every Suffolk alive today can trace its ancestry to one stallion, Crisp's Horse of Ufford, which was foaled in 1760. They are always chestnut in colour and are comparatively short in the leg, reaching about seventeen hands, but with powerful compact bodies and a beautiful crest on the neck. They were bred for row-crop work on the heavy soils of the eastern counties where cash crops have always been important. They therefore have small neat feet and clean legs with little feather. These factors tended to make them ideal for producing weight-carrying hunters when crossed with a thoroughbred stallion. The high demand for such hunters in the last thirty years has meant that fewer and fewer mares have been bred pure, and numbers have thus declined alarmingly.

The last breed, but by no means the least, is a more recent import to this country, the Percheron, brought over from France during the First World War. Originally from the old La Perche district of France, they have been exported to many countries and have become the most popular heavy horse in the world. In fact the Mexican word for heavy working horse is 'Percheronne'. They are similar in shape, conformation and size to the Suffolk, also being commonest in the eastern counties. They are always dark dapple-grey or black with clean legs devoid of feather and small black hooves which are extremely hard-wearing. They have deep short bodies, a high crest over the neck and a pretty and aristocratic head. Although they are a minor breed in this country, new blood can always be reintroduced from the continent ensuring their safe survival.

So what of the future? Are the numbers of cart horses going to continue to decline and the few remaining be reserved for brewers' drays in the show ring? I think not. I believe that with the increased cost of fuel and machinery we are on the brink of a heavy horse revival. I have strong indications that there is renewed interest from the agricultural industry. Many farmers, particularly those with a small acreage of arable, are looking to the professional contractor to do those jobs which require large, expensive, specialised machines. Many of the remaining jobs could be done equally well, or in some cases better, by horses, particularly in marginal areas with a high percentage of steep hillside. But if the demand returns too quickly, there will be a very real problem of supply.

First let us take the basic power unit, the horse itself. Since the rapid decline of the cart horse after the Second World War, breeders have found it more and more difficult to make a profit. Most of the foals they bred would almost certainly have ended up in the meat trade. Fortunately this does not pay well enough in Britain, and cart mares were therefore kept barren.

The only customers prepared to pay a good price for young horses were the breweries, for their show teams, and the breeders selected their breeding stock accordingly. It was a market that required big horses, the bigger the better. They had to be high-stepping and showy, with, of course, four white feet. They obviously had to have a reliable temperament and be easy to train, but these two vital attributes tended to be deemed less important than the others. They would never be handled by one man on his own, unassisted. They would not have to stand in one place hitched to a cart for long periods of time. They would not have to work, regardless of the weather, up to their hocks in mud. Nor was the cost of their feed a very important consideration.

The Ardennes breed of working horse, ideal for many of today's farms. Charles Pinney gives instruction in their handling at one of the courses held on Joe Henson's farm.

In other words, the breeders were re-creating the large, high-stepping, fiery war horse from which our farm horses were descended; they were good at their job and it did not take them long. If you ask a farmer what he needs to cart his pig dung, a war horse or a pudd'n – the answer's 'a pudd'n'. But where are the old farm pudd'ns of yesteryear? Gone for ever. And what is available to the farmer at a price he can afford? Only the brewery rejects – the war horses that did not quite make the grade. Can you think of anything less suitable to cart home the hay than bad, unreliable war horses? I certainly can't. Our beef breeders who bred their cattle in one direction for a small, fat, early maturing beast, almost bred the legs off their animals, then had to import stock from the continent when the demand changed, almost over-night, in favour of a large lean carcase. So also our horse breeders will have to look to the continent, where the work horse is still important, for the small, reliable, highly trainable horse which is inexpensive to buy and cheap to keep.

The relatively 'unimproved' Ardennes breed from France, with its small compact body, muscular hind-quarters, black legs, and hooves as hard as iron, is the breed I am putting my money on and into. These horses had to be worked by the women and children when the men were away fighting in the wars which France seems to have been continually mixed up in. They are therefore, by necessity, extremely docile and those which were not were eaten! The French, unlike us, have no qualms about that. The Ardennes' small size – they rarely go above 15.2 hands – makes them cheap to feed. Why fuel a 100 h.p. tractor when a 50 h.p. one will do. Being low to the ground on their short strong legs increases the efficiency of draught. All their strength is used to pull the plough through the soil, not lift it out; you hitch a plough behind the axle of a tractor not to the top of the cab.

But the Ardennes' most important asset is undoubtedly its docile temperament. The French have still got a wealth of sleepy old pudd'ns. Regrettably, many of them are bred for meat – a profitable industry in France – for, as with humans, it is the quiet docile individuals that fatten best. The French require lean meat and this means muscle. Let us once again put this muscle to work to help us out of our energy crisis. The only apparent disadvantage of the Ardennes is its colour; some are bay but most are a light strawberry roan. Will the English market resist this strange colour? Many cattle dealers foretold that we would never accept the yellow Charolais, but we did. If we can accept custard-coloured cattle, why not horses the colour of blancmange?

The next problem facing the would-be user of working horses is acquiring suitable machinery for them to pull. The leading manufacturers of farm machinery in this country have long since ceased to produce horse-drawn equipment. Those who are still doing so on a small scale are aiming their product at the under-developed countries where soil conditions and draught animals are quite different. Here, if you want horse-drawn equipment suited to our soil, you have to buy rusty machines which have spent the last thirty years lying in someone's nettle patch. You also have to pay an inflated price, bidding against antique dealers whose customers are the farm museums which are springing up like mushrooms, or landlords of pubs called 'The Plough', 'The Harrow' or 'The Hay Wain'. Needless to say there is no after-sales service with these purchases. Once again we must turn to the continent for modern equipment and look to a country like Poland, where the horse is still the most common and most important power unit of agriculture. When a market has been created in this country, maybe British machinery manufacturers will again turn their thoughts and their skill to the world of the horse.

If we are looking at new equipment made of modern materials and designed with modern technology, maybe we should be bringing our harness up to date too. Apart from the show sets, the best harness you see today is not hanging in the farm tack room, it's hanging in the lounge bar – and some antique dealer has made a fat profit getting it there. How can the small farmer possibly compete at harness sales and does he really need shining leather harness with brass fittings? It takes far longer to clean than it does to get dirty. Now we are really stepping on hallowed ground! Dare one suggest nylon webbing and plastic straps, with stainless steel buckles, which can be dropped in a bucket of soapy water and hung up to dry? Well, if I am using horses to help clean out my pigs and not to win the Royal Show, I know which I would prefer.

The final and seemingly unobtainable commodity that the newcomer to the working horse cannot start without is expertise. If you have never tacked up a horse, or shut one into a cart, how do you begin? The obvious answer is to seek the help and guidance of the oldest inhabitant at the 'local'. He will shake his head knowingly but kindly and try to explain to the hapless enthusiast that, to understand cart horses, you have to be 'born among 'em'. He will then start talking in a foreign language, using words like 'Forrard 'un', 'Wan-tee' and 'Ames'. I must confess that I used the last word for ten years before I saw it in print for the first time and learnt that it begins with an 'h'.

All of this has a ring of truth and might well put the forward-thinking new-comer off before he even starts to make plans. It's true that you cannot become an experienced carter overnight, but the same applies to becoming a tractor driver, and however kind you are to a tractor it will never help you when you get into trouble. Anyone with a love and understanding of animals, and most livestock farmers have that or they would not be in the business, will be able to crack the horse job given the basic principles. My friend and partner, Charles Pinney, satisfies this need. At the time of writing, he is the only instructor employed by the Agricultural Training Board to teach the handling of heavy horses. His four-day residential courses here at the Cotswold Farm Park are in such demand that applicants have to join a waiting list of up to three months. Orders for our Polish horse equipment and Ardennes horses are also building up. Is this merely a reflection of the 'good life' syndrome? Is it just a harking back to the days of our youth when we lay in the new-mown hay and watched the horses silently and contentedly going about their work? Admittedly, after a day's tractor driving it takes several cups of tea to wash the taste of diesel fumes from my throat and several hours for my ears to get used to being without their sound protectors, but I sincerely believe that there is more to it than that. A change of plan has to make real economic sense before being accepted by hard-headed farmers working to survive, and I am as hard-headed as the next.

Was it a coincidence that British agriculture boomed during the heyday of the working horse? Is it a coincidence that, although farming is Britain's largest industry, by whatever standards you care to adopt it is now looked upon as the poor relation of British industry and has been struggling to survive ever since it dropped the cart horse in favour of greedy engines? I wonder if our farming will ever lead the world again and, if so, if it will ride back into prosperity on the backs of the Gentle Giants which served it so well in the golden days gone by.

Thank Goodness for Tractors

TED MOULT

Sitting in my quiet cab the other evening, working the last field down ready for sowing with winter wheat, I was reflecting on the differences between the style of operations then and now – then being in the horse age, which was still extant when I started my farming career.

In the first place, I wouldn't have been doing it at all at that time. With horses, operations ceased when the birds went to bed. Horses only did overtime in the summer and, even then, needed regular feeds since they cannot be filled up like camels for long trips between scattered fuel dumps. Secondly, I wouldn't have been listening to *Any Questions* – only to the wind in the trees, the jangle of the harness, plus the random call of crow, cock pheasant, or whatever bird happened to be in attendance.

It must be about twelve years since the number of horses was counted in this country. I was thinking about this omission when I filled in my agricultural census returns recently. Not that the Ministry of Agriculture, Fisheries and Food asks fewer questions on animals in general: there are categories such as 'Irish stores', Gilts in-pig, Ewe lambs put to the ram, Poultry excluding game-birds, and many more. But the section marked 'Horses' is no longer with us. Its purpose then had been to give an assessment of the actual pulling force on the land, supplied first by oxen, then by horses, and finally by steam engines and tractors. I suppose the counting stopped when real horse power changed to h.p.; although h.p. is itself now a meaningless term, being supplanted by Brake Horse Power. The importance of machinery in the census is emphasised by the section on tractors, some of which 'is required by the EEC under regulation'. This seeks information in precise detail and takes up at least half a page.

Still, horses munch grass and eat hay, and it is unfortunate that the official statistics now pass over this vital information. If one could count the total number of horses, I am sure it would be an all-time record. (Judging by what one can see in the peripheral urban areas it is almost at pollution level!) The provision of fodder, especially after a dry summer as in 1975 and 1976, can be mighty costly – 'Feeding Smokey can take all Philippa's pocket money.'

Ted Moult and Angela Rippon discovered this traditional working horse at a farm museum, now often the only place to see real horse-power.

Although the work horse population of our farms sank to the lowest figure in history in the early 1960s – I think it was in 1960 that only twenty mares and fillies were registered with the Shire Horse Society – the funny thing is that the number of heavy horses has risen dramatically since that time, but no more horses are ploughing or pulling carts than twenty years ago. The increase in interest was demonstrated in the 1979 Foal Stakes held at the Staffordshire Show Ground. At the sale the foals averaged about £500 and some prize winners made up to 3000 guineas. In 1960 a foal would only make about £25, probably for hamburgers, with just a few die-hard horse enthusiasts taking notice, whereas at Stafford you couldn't see the animals for people.

There are some who assert that the day of the horse as a worker will return, and indeed there are a few farmers, conspicuous by their scarcity, who boast of doing all the chores by Dobbin power. One fancies, however, that such people probably make more money out of showing, demonstrating or hiring out the horses than they do from farming. (I once interviewed a Sussex hurdle maker who admitted that talking about hurdles was more rewarding than making them. In any case the sheep were folded on the turnips with either wire or electrified netting.) Horses are supposed to be economical, or so some breweries claim as they deliver beer with two magnificent Shires decked out with brasses, bobs in their plaited manes. A good advertisement, too.

There may be a few horse-drawn vehicles on farms, but I can only think of one within a twenty-mile radius of where I live. Apart from this the only man near here who drives a horse is my ex-cowman who exchanged milk for beer by joining a brewery on leaving the land a few years ago, and who has a pony and trap, purely for pleasure.

Two years ago the local ploughing match was held on my place. Plenty of tractors but not one team of horses arrived. It was rumoured that some might have put in an appearance had cash incentives been forthcoming. A pity, I thought, recalling my own experiences in that direction, for as a youth (under eighteen) I entered myself for the Lads' Class with a pair of trusty nags. It was soon obvious to me that some horses were there for the ploughing and some for the Horse Show which followed, but to qualify for the latter they had to enter the former. If an animal is in show condition it is unlikely to walk nice and steady, either in a straight line down the furrow or on the land. It will probably jump about, snatching at the collar in fits and starts, walking all over the place, so that another man is needed to lead it. Here's a tip. Never wrap the plough line round your thumbs. If a vital link breaks up front, the horses thus liberated from the plough go like hell, and you go with them ... very nasty!

Looking back on any period of one's life is a tricky pastime. One tends to become nostalgic, maybe for lost youth, but in the main, I suggest, because the mind favours the pleasant bits while rejecting the rest – a kind of self-adjusting mechanism. Moreover to many contemporaries, ignorant of the day-to-day reality of the pre-tractor (or part-tractor in my case) era, life then must seem to have been a gentle rural idyll smelling of linseed oil and bran.

Well, it wasn't so. The term work horse means what it says. They worked. Some would now be called workaholics. Being a noble creature a horse will try and try again, unlike a mule which has a built-in regulator on its throttle when it reaches optimum effort. A sight not to be missed was a timber merchant's string of powerful animals teaming a heavily laden timber drag out of the woods with a concerted effort that would do the England Rugby forwards credit. As the saying goes: 'Horses sweat, men perspire, while ladies merely glow', and as far as horses are concerned it's certainly true.

In the summer, grass mowing used sometimes to start at first light (in spite of the fact that the grass cut when still wet with dew would take longer to make into hay than grass cut dry) to enable the horses to work in the cool. When I took horses to plough, the practice was to walk to the field, hook up the team in the morning and remain there until knocking off at about three in the afternoon. Instead of having a dinner break when the animals (sweating, of course) might get cold, I used to eat one sandwich then plough another round. Four sandwiches – four stops.

When the four-legged workers were stabled and fed they were covered in hay and coarse hessian sacks until they had stopped steaming and were dry enough to be turned out for the night. Sometimes I had to sit up late to do this. It was better to turn them out than keep them in unless they were doing extra hard graft.

One of the problems that had to be coped with was a disease known as 'grease', a thickening of the skin with suppurating sores in the heel of the hind leg, especially common in very hairy or besom-legged animals. It occurred mostly if they were standing about too much, over a weekend for example, and particularly if the horse was receiving too much corn. Hence the saying 'He can't take his corn'. Often you could hear a horse stamping his foot with irritation for hours on end. Today, with antibiotics, this condition would be easily dealt with; in those days some of the bizarre palliatives used included urine (hotted up) and tractor sump oil – crude antiseptics, at best.

When I started work, many acres of cereals were actually sown by hand, out of a hopper hung round the neck. The first bit of broadcasting that I ever did was not on any particular wavelength, but by casting handfuls of seed wheat on to the ground. There is more to this, however, than just hurling the stuff to the floor. You have to get a rhythm going between your hands and feet, and cunningly discard a proportion of your handful as you bring your hand out of the hopper and then spread the rest, opening the hand as you return it to the container. If you are successful no ground will be missed.

These days most fields of wheat, barley and oats are planted with a corn-drill, the operator floating about in a comfortable, quiet cab (under ninety decibels) with air conditioning, radio or stereo cassette, and a luxury seat. Maybe there will be a two-way radio at some future date? Since agriculture has changed from a labour intensive to a capital-intensive industry, the theory has been accepted that, if a man on the land is happy and relaxed, his output, dependent on h.p. at-the-elbow rather than muscle power, will improve.

By contrast, I remember, years ago, seeing a farmworker protected from the elements simply by a thick bran bag round his shoulders fastened by a natty six-inch nail. He was standing on a tractor pulling a mowing machine and cutting thistles in the cow pasture. A standard job on wet summer days before herbicides were available.

> *Cut a thistle in May, up next day,*
> *Cut a thistle in June, up again soon,*
> *Cut a thistle in July, then it's sure to die.*

On that day, the rain was coming down in stair rods, but there was no seat on the tractor! 'Why don't you buy your man a seat?' I asked. 'I don't pay my men to sit down,' said the old fool.

The first machine I had anything to do with was a pre-war Fordson, a bone-shaker on spade lugs. For road work you had road-bands – even more bone-shaking. There was no such thing as a starter motor; you had to swing the cranking handle from the front – just the job to give yourself a double hernia on a cold morning. In fact by the time the engine had started you had generated enough heat to last at least until lunchtime. (This model was, curiously enough, quite warm due to its solid mudguards and to the low position of the driver relative to the centre of gravity.) Another complication was that the machine ran on paraffin but petrol was needed for starting it.

A further hazard was the advance and retard control for the ignition. The clutch and the brake were combined in one pedal, which could be secured by a hook attached to the footplate. This was especially dangerous when pulling a converted horse-drawn mowing machine which was driven by a land wheel, as this wheel only needed to roll forward an inch or two to activate the reciprocating knife between the fingers of the cutter bar. You had to watch out for your own fingers.

There is no doubt that the great step forward was the invention by Harry Ferguson of the hydraulic system. He found that instead of merely dragging implements, his three-point linkage would actually pick them up off the ground and put them down again. He then found that due to the close-coupled position of the implements, the greater the draught the greater became the grip or traction of the rear wheels. This was achieved by a clever method of transferring the weight to the back axle through the top link. This was un-doubtedly the biggest boon to all land workers since the invention of the well-ington boot, since at the end of a day's work all that needed to be done was to lift up the plough and whizz home, without the bore of having to unhitch the thing or lift it on to a trolley or land wheels.

The more a tractor pulls, the more its front end is lifted up – indeed one of the most frequent causes of death on the farm was being crushed by a rearing tractor fastened to some resistant object such as a tree stump. (The rope should always be fastened as low as possible, near the centre of gravity.) Therefore as implements became heavier weights had to be added to the front. In modern tractors this principle is now exploited to such an extent that very often the total sum of the weights, plus the ballast from water in the tyres, approaches the weight of the machine that is carrying them. It was then found that pushing the front wheels through a lot of loose soil gave a degree of rolling resistance, hence the development of the four-wheel-drive models. This is not the com-plete answer, since, as the front wheels rotate slightly faster than the rear, on certain light soils they fragment the surface, causing wheel-slip at the back.

Many jobs have disappeared altogether. Threshing the corn, so nostalgically presented in farm museums, is one. That's where it should be. All dust, dirt, and killing vermin. Carting coal to the steam engine is another. Carrying eighteen stone of wheat in a railway bag was not so bad if you were strong enough, but a bit rough if you had to walk up steps to the loft as well. Lifting by hand is now seldom demanded, thanks to elevators, hydraulic loaders and lifters. It's funny that people still have bad backs – it must be because they sit awkwardly.

My first experience of making silage was throwing the grass on to a horse-drawn dray and then forking it into a round concrete silo. This primitive method must seem barely credible to the current operators of modern forage equipment.

With the techniques now readily available we have the ability to farm all types of land according to the dictates of external political and economic factors. But the search for increased food production must go on, whatever the short-term prospects of surpluses seem to be. It will be a race between technology, energy supplies, and population.

In the meantime, thank goodness for tractors, I say. I only wish I knew more about how to maintain 'em!

The Charcoal Burner

BERNARD PRICE

Legend has it that it was a charcoal burner who picked up the abandoned body of William Rufus, killed by an arrow while hunting in the New Forest, and carried it by cart to Winchester, thereby saving it from 'crow, dog and and vermin'.

Charcoal burning was always something of a secret craft, the place of work more often betrayed by smell rather than sight. The basic method of making charcoal barely changed in Britain from the Conquest until the Second World War. In that time the lifestyle of the charcoal burner, or 'wood-collier' as he was once known, had changed but little. The traditional form of pole-frame hut was used by many families until well into this century. Metal kilns were found to be highly suitable during the thirties and were able to fulfil the renewed demand for charcoal through the war years. The last charcoal burner to earn his living with log-built, earth-sealed kilns continued until 1948.

Expert kiln building was vital to the success of any charcoal enterprise. The burning of the wood to create the charcoal must be slow and controlled, achieved by restricting the air supply. The result is a carbon that makes an excellent fuel, since charcoal generates double the heat of its equivalent weight in wood. It was extensively used in the past for smelting metal, and is still used for various processes within the metal industry today. As an ingredient it has long been used in the production of gunpowder, glass, soap, biscuits, shoe-black, ink, crayons, batteries, and much else. Charcoal has always been widely used as a filter for air and water, and the by-products of charcoal have many and varied uses in modern industry. Because of this most charcoal burning has now left the forest glade and become a wholly industrial process, presided over in continuous retort factories by chemists and technicians.

About eight years ago I was lucky enough to meet a married couple who had been among the last of the charcoal burners. They told me how they made

Above: In the heart of the forest, a wooden kiln ready for firing.

Below: Up to three days later, the pit is raked and any remaining dust and earth used as a final seal for the next kiln.

their kilns with wood stacked to form a triangular-shaped central flue about three and a half feet high. The wood to be charred was laid around it and was covered in turn with small bits of wood about an inch in diameter. Finely sieved earth and dust from the hearth of earlier burnings gave the final seal before the kiln was fired with burning embers which were fed into the flue. The kilns varied in size according to the quantity of wood to be charred and there were regional differences in the construction of the kilns. A kiln might take three days and two nights to burn, and throughout that time it would be carefully watched and the ventilation controlled.

The two charcoal burners who talked to me told of a life spent in camps of turf huts built like Indian tepees, the framework covered with sacks and turf. Small huts were bedrooms, while a larger one provided the living area, complete with table and a chest to hold clothes. Cooking was done over an open fire or in an oven made from a metal box set in an earth bank. They told me that they always ate well, and that their only real problem was keeping their clothes dry in heavy rain. It is a way of life unthought of by a generation who now purchase their charcoal from the supermarket in handy packs in order to fire their garden barbecues.

Chalk Marks

BERNARD PRICE

I was ten years old when my father died of his wounds during the Second World War, and it was then that I discovered the South Downs and found my spiritual home. I walked eighteen miles on that hot summer's day of 1944, and gasped at the sheer sweeping beauty of the valleys and the bounding energy of the rolling hills. When I arrived back home that evening I fell on my bed fully clothed and slept till morning. There were so many things I had seen that day but not understood, and from that time on, when not in school, I devoted myself to exploring the countryside, learning all I could of its formation and the living creatures and history that lay within it.

As the years have gone by so my enthusiasm for all Downland has increased, and I am ever aware of its many unsolved mysteries, particularly those relating to early man. Some of the most profound of these are the great hillside figures cut into the chalk. As my old friend Andrew Young, pastor and poet, once wrote of the Long Man of Wilmington:

> *What figure, drawn in chalk, strides with his pole*
> *Across the Downs, as naked as a soul?*
> *Odin or Balder? Time will solve the doubt*
> *And mail clad robots look on a Boy Scout.*

It was as a Boy Scout that I once ate lunch sitting on the Long Man's head while speculating upon his origins. Indeed, speculation and conjecture have come to play a large part in what has been written over the years concerning these figures. During the nineteenth century many were regarded as being either the work of 'Ancient Britons' or memorials of King Alfred's victory over the Danes. Many are in fact no more than rather charming follies of the eighteenth and nineteenth centuries; there are but few of truly ancient origin and, in my opinion, the most important of these are the Long Man of Wilmington, the Uffington White Horse, and the Cerne Giant.

They raise many questions. Who cut these intaglio figures into the chalk? Who or what do they represent and what was their significance? Identification and dating is difficult enough; for the answers to other questions we need to turn our attention to the studies made into folklore and folk memory.

The Long Man of Wilmington is situated some three miles north of Eastbourne and south of the Brighton to Hastings road. It is one of the largest portrayals of a human figure in the world and is magnificently situated on the steep face of Windover Hill. The Long Man is easily viewed from the road, although at 500 feet above sea level his head is quite frequently in the clouds or shrouded in mist. As the old Sussex couplet has it:

> *When Firle or Long Man wears a cap,*
> *We in the valley gets a drap.*

The Long Man is a slim and rather elegant figure, standing with his feet apart and holding a staff in each hand. He is 231 feet high and measures 115 feet between the staves. Such proportions must have been the result of much thought and planning, for the perspective is remarkable. The earliest mention of the Long Man is to be found in the Burrell manuscripts of 1779 which include a drawing showing the two staves as a rake and a scythe respectively. The original outline of the figure was merely a shallow trench, which made it difficult to see unless the sunlight fell obliquely upon it. It also stood out boldly in winter when the snow hung in the outline trench during a thaw. The seventh Duke of Devonshire, who had so firmly put his stamp on the landscape with the building of Eastbourne in the 1860s, caused the restoration of the giant figure by having the outline marked with bricks. In 1925 responsibility for the figure was conveyed to the Sussex Archaeological Society which now carries out repairs and whitewashing. Such figures are as enigmatic as the Sphinx of Egypt. Could it be that the Wilmington Giant, as the Long Man is often called, is no more than the fanciful whim of some eighteenth-century squire or farmer? If this were so, one would have expected the indefatigable Burrell to have learned something of it when he was collecting information in the late eighteenth century. Nor is there any reason to suppose it to be the work of medieval monks from the nearby Wilmington Priory, which was at one time suggested.

The solution to the problem posed by this particular figure may well be contained in the fascinating account I read, in March 1965, of the discovery of a three-inch bronze buckle in a Saxon grave at Finglesham, near Deal. Cast in low relief on the buckle plate is a curious figure bearing extraordinary similarities to the Long Man of Wilmington. Both figures are naked and their feet turn to the right in what could be a form of ritual step. Professor C. F. C. Hawkes, then Professor of European Archaeology at Oxford University,

The Long Man of Wilmington – one of the largest portrayals of the human figure in the world. Was the Giant simply the fanciful whim of some eighteenth-century squire?

suggested that the Long Man or Wilmington Giant might be a disarmed figure of the Germanic war-god Woden, worshipped in Scandinavia as Odin; which says much for the astonishing omniscience of Andrew Young. Professor Hawkes also suggested that the disarming of the Long Man might have been carried out on the instructions of St Wilfrid, the apostle of Sussex, in the seventh century.

Like the nineteenth-century naturalist Richard Jefferies, I never omit to explore a footpath, for never was there a footpath which did not pass something of interest. I must confess that I have never made special journeys to see any of the hill figures of which I write; it is simply that I have come upon them on the many walks I have made across considerable areas of Britain over the past twenty-five years. It may be that this is the best way to discover them; I certainly believe so. It was while walking the Ridgeway Path, from Ivinghoe in Hertfordshire to Avebury in Wiltshire, the very heart of hill-figure country, that I had my first sight of the Uffington White Horse. This symbolic figure resembles no conventional horse, and it stretches itself across the hill with all the sensuality of an impressionist drawing. Unlike the Long Man it appears to offer itself to the sky rather than the surrounding countryside, but it can, in fact, be seen from well over ten miles away. The Uffington Horse hangs like a magical amulet at the throat of White Horse Hill, and also gives its name to the Vale of the White Horse. Poised between Swindon and Wantage, this is the landscape so well known to Thomas Hughes, who lived in the village of Uffington and is celebrated as the author of *Tom Brown's Schooldays*. He also wrote *The Scouring of the White Horse* which tells how this chalk mark was once cleaned every seven years, an occasion for fairs and great revelry.

The surrounding landscape is a rich and fitting complement to such a wondrous animal, full of history and steeped in legend. The Iron Age hill fort that surmounts White Horse Hill with its massive earth ramparts is known as Uffington Castle. Visitors from all over the world come to see the chalk figure, which is undoubtedly one of the wonders of Europe, but the name of Uffington Castle frequently causes confusion as tourists search in vain for some pile of mildewed masonry. Below this northern escarpment of the Berkshire Downs is the strange flat-topped chalk hillock where St George is said

Uffington's ancient yet contemporary-looking horse, seen from the air. Its extraordinary shape was probably inspired by coins used in that part of southern Britain in the first century B.C. (below) which had been copied from the gold staters of Philip II of Macedon (above).

to have slain the dragon. A short walk westwards along the Ridgeway will bring you to Wayland's Smithy, the name given to a Neolithic chambered longbarrow much renowned in story and song. It is said that here the shoes were made for the Uffington White Horse.

Yet what of the Horse? The first written record of it was made in the twelfth century with the mention of White Horse Hill, and in the fourteenth century the Horse is described as being second only to Stonehenge in terms of interest. The antiquarians of the eighteenth century, mostly doctors, squires, and clergymen, began to take great interest in the early hill figures, and arguments and attributions flew as thick as gnats. In our own century G. K. Chesterton used poetic licence to go far beyond the limits of possibility in his 'Ballad of the White Horse':

> *Before the gods that made the gods*
> *Had seen their sunrise pass,*
> *The White Horse of the White Horse Vale,*
> *Was cut out of the grass.*

Most authorities now consider that the Horse dates from the same pre-Roman period as Uffington Castle itself. The cult of the horse was common in ancient history and in some ways it has continued through to the present day. White is traditionally the most noble colour for a horse. We find in the description of the Apocalypse in *Revelation* that it is the white horse that is symbolical of victory and triumph. From Tacitus we learn that the German tribes kept milk-white horses in consecrated woods and groves. Virgil also noted that white horses were not usually put to work, for they were beloved of the gods and it was considered criminal to wound or kill such an animal except for sacrifice. A white horse appeared on the standard of the Saxons, in the arms of Saxony and of the House of Brunswick. Today it is common as an inn sign.

The Uffington White Horse is the largest of Britain's hillside horses, 360 feet long and 130 feet high at its tallest part, and it probably inspired the other more naturalistic horses. Its own extraordinary shape was probably inspired by early coins used in the area in the first century B.C., which carried debased representations of the horse on the gold stater of Philip II of Macedon, the father of Alexander the Great. Other unusual horse-like figures can be observed in the metalwork of late Celtic ornament, on bucket mountings in particular.

The seven-year cycle of festivities, so lovingly described by Thomas Hughes, that once kept the Uffington Horse clean has now long gone. Once it was the responsibility of the Lord of the Manor to feed and entertain the 'scourers', who all came from the local villages and considered it their duty to do the work. The tradition lapsed, however, and by 1880 the Horse had become overgrown. Now it is expertly groomed by the Department of the Environment – which to me seems somehow like obtaining folklore on the National Health.

A county that never fails to surprise me with the variety of its landscape, wildlife and antiquities is Dorset. My walks in that county have led me through a Purbeck stone quarry in the footsteps of a dinosaur, and while in Hardy country I have enjoyed the works of the great writer and the landscape that so inspired him. Also in Dorset is a hillside that displays one of the most extraordinary monuments I know, the club-wielding figure of the Cerne Giant. I first came upon it when I had walked up from Dorchester while heading for Blackmore Vale, and suddenly, at Cerne Abbas, was confronted and startled by the Giant, who overlooks the A352 between Dorchester and Sherborne. The figure has been described as the 'most remarkable portrait in Bri-

The Cerne Giant, although smaller than his counterpart at Wilmington, is memorable for his masculinity. It is difficult to understand how this pagan figure remained intact so close to the Abbey.

tain of male aggressiveness and sexual energy' and quite clearly was intended as a symbol of strength and fertility. The Cerne Giant, with his carefully emphasised ribs and great phallus, is very different from the Long Man of Wilmington, who appears sexless and lacks the physical bulk and muscle of his Dorset counterpart, although he is taller.

The Cerne Giant is 180 feet high and is supposed to represent Hercules, a suggestion that was first put forward in the eighteenth century. The cutting does not have the freedom of line so apparent in the Uffington Horse; this indicates a later date and it may well be that the origins of the Cerne Giant are Romano-British, which would explain the association with Hercules.

What is difficult to understand, however, is why such a very pagan figure was left undisturbed when it was situated so near to an abbey. It may be that its relevance as a symbol of fertility was too important to the local population for it to be removed. Today most people regard the Giant with some affection, and it is by no means unknown for it still to be visited by childless couples.

A number of hill figures well known in past centuries have since disappeared, but in some instances a study of crop marks and resistivity surveys has yielded important new information that could lead in the future to some 'lost' figures being re-cut. Of the thirty or so known hill figures in Britain, only a handful are to be found in the North. The richest harvest of horses and other marks occurs in Wiltshire and about its borders, yet wherever they are to be found you may be certain they have a story to tell, of pre-history, history, or sheer eccentricity. In the words of Edward Thomas:

Was there a man once who straddled across
The back of the Westbury White Horse
Over there on Salisbury Plain's green wall?
Was he bound for Westbury, or had he a fall?
The swift, the swallow, the hawk and the hern.
There are two million things for me to learn.

Provided that we do not neglect them, or destroy them with the weight of our enthusiastic feet, the hill figures will remain for generations to come. For my own part I look forward to finding continued enjoyment in walking, and to understanding better the story of Britain and the countryside. Whenever I come upon the great hill figures I pause, wonder, and greet them like old friends. I hope you will too.

Chalk Marks

White Horse of Strichen
White Stag of Strichen
Kilburn Horse
Whiteleaf Cross
Bledlow Cross
Alton Barnes Horse
Watlington White Mark
Whipsnade White Lion
Marlborough Horse
Broad Town Horse
Bulford Kiwi
Hackpen Horse
Uffington White Horse
Cherhill Horse
Laverstock Panda
Westbury Horse
Pewsey New Horse
Wiltshire Regimental Badges
Woolbury Horse
Wye Crown
Cerne Giant
Long Man of Wilmington
Osmington Horse
Litlington Horse
Ditchling Cross

Horses

Aberdeenshire
White Horse of Strichen This horse was cut by the Fraser family in the late eighteenth century or early nineteenth century on Mormond Hill, twelve miles from Peterhead.

Berkshire
Uffington White Horse The most celebrated and largest of all the white horses, probably cut during the first century B.C.

Dorset
Osmington Horse This is the only horse with a rider still visible, and was cut early in the nineteenth century. The rider is George III, and he and his horse face out over Weymouth Bay.

Hampshire
Woolbury Horse This small and crudely constructed horse at Woolbury Camp near Stockbridge is believed to represent the horse of a local highwayman. It was probably cut in the late eighteenth century, possibly later.

Sussex
Litlington Horse This horse, cut on Hindover Hill at Litlington, near Seaford, can be seen from Beachy Head. It dates from about 1925 and replaces an earlier horse cut in 1838.

Wiltshire
Alton Barnes Horse A good-looking horse, cut in 1812 at the instigation of Robert Pile of the Manor Farm, Alton Barnes.
Broad Town Horse This horse, between Swindon and Avebury, is believed to have been cut in 1864 but may have originated earlier in the century.
Cherhill Horse Situated east of Avebury, the Cherhill Horse was cut by Dr Alsop of Calne in 1780. He gave orders to his workmen on Cherhill Down by shouting through a megaphone from the village. Originally the horse had a glass eye made of old bottles but they were all stolen within a hundred years.
Hackpen Horse This horse is on the face of Hackpen Hill overlooking Winterbourne Bassett, and is believed to have been cut to mark the Coronation of Queen Victoria in 1838.
Marlborough Horse This small horse, difficult to see at ground level, was cut by boys from Greasley's Academy, Marlborough, on Granham Hill in 1804.
Pewsey New Horse Cut on Pewsey Hill on the outskirts of Pewsey by George Marples in 1937, this horse commemorated the Coronation of George VI.
Westbury Horse The Westbury Horse, on Bratton Down some two miles from

Westbury, was cut early in the eighteenth century. The horse was remodelled in 1778, when its outline was drastically altered.

Yorkshire
Kilburn Horse In the right weather conditions this horse on the Hambleton Hills near Kilburn may be seen from York. It was cut in 1857 and almost wiped out in 1896 by a severe hailstorm.

Giants

Dorset
Cerne Giant The renowned and shameless Romano-British fertility symbol representing Hercules overlooks the village of Cerne Abbas.

Sussex
Long Man of Wilmington Also called the Wilmington Giant, the Long Man is 231 feet high and possibly dates from the Saxon period. The outline has been subjected to alterations over the centuries.

Crosses

Buckinghamshire
Bledlow Cross This cross is a landmark in the Vale of Aylesbury, but its viewing points are limited. Its origin is uncertain but it may date from the eighteenth century.
Whiteleaf Cross This is another landmark of far greater prominence overlooking the Icknield Way near Monks Risborough and possibly medieval in origin.

Sussex
Ditchling Cross Situated on the Downs about five miles from Lewes on the road to Plumpton, this cross may be associated with the Battle of Lewes in 1264.

Other Hill Figures

Aberdeenshire
White Stag of Strichen Cut in 1870 by an architect named Gardner, the White Stag covers almost an acre of ground on the opposite side of Mormond Hill to the White Horse.

Bedfordshire
Whipsnade White Lion The White Lion on the Dunstable Downs below Whipsnade Zoo was cut in 1935 and measures 483 feet from nose to tail.

Kent

Wye Crown This crown, which marks the Coronation of Edward VII, was cut in 1902 by students of Wye College a mile from Wye on the North Downs.

Oxfordshire

Watlington White Mark This obelisk was cut in 1764 on Watlington Hill, and is now National Trust property.

Wiltshire

Regimental Badges The badges can be clearly seen from the A30 some ten miles west of Salisbury, and were cut by soldiers of various regiments stationed in the area during the First World War.

Bulford Kiwi This bird, on Beacon Hill near Bulford, Salisbury Plain, is 420 feet long and was cut by troops from New Zealand during the First World War.

Laverstock Panda A panda's head 55 feet by 40 feet situated about a mile from Salisbury on the Exeter road. It was cut in 1969, and was probably the work of students.

The Kilburn horse on the Hambleton Hills in Yorkshire – one of the few white horses in the north of England.

The Cricket Bat Maker

BERNARD PRICE

In spite of Mr Kerry Packer's new look for the international game of cricket, the old game as played on hundreds of village greens throughout the summer remains, for millions of people, one of the most evocative images of the English countryside. During 1979 an aluminium cricket bat was flourished for the first time in a test match and it must have seemed like heresy to the traditional cricket bat makers; for them there can be no substitute for the willow blade.

One of the great firms I know, at Robertsbridge in East Sussex, has been making cricket bats since 1875, although their founder was making bats for himself and friends much earlier than that.

Willow is the main raw material used and, although there are many different varieties of willow, the most suitable for cricket bats is *Salix alba caerulea*. These willows can grow to a height of a hundred feet and up to eighteen feet in girth. Another vital material is cane for the handles which is imported from the East Indies; the best cane is known as Sarawak. Both the willow and the cane are light, tough, and highly resilient.

Growing the willow is an art in itself. Cuttings known in the trade as setts, free of knots and blemishes, are first grown to a height of twelve feet. The timber is extremely fast growing and setts need plenty of room when planted out in plantation rows. Such trees require protection from rabbits and cattle, and all shoots and buds are rubbed from the trunk to a height of ten feet. Trees are ready for cricket bat making when they have a circumference of fifty inches when measured five feet from the ground. Twelve-year-old cricket bat willows are a very profitable crop.

When felled the tree is cut into lengths of two feet four inches. These are split lengthwise with the grain, using wooden wedges, into sections known as clefts, and each cleft will make a blade. After very rough shaping the clefts are graded and stacked for seasoning, a process that takes between nine and twelve months.

The next stage is to shape the blade further, giving it the correct width and the familiar face and back. In order that it may withstand the impact of a cricket ball, the blade undergoes the first of three pressings, being passed through a shaped roller at a pressure of about two tons per square inch.

Sarawak cane is cut into handle lengths and, after further grading and sorting, these are split by a machine which planes the sides of the cane flat enabling the pieces to be glued together. Insertions of cork or rubber are also added to the handle to absorb the shock of impact when the bat is used. The handle is then turned for shape and one end is wedge cut for fitting into the blade. The handle is held only by glue and a perfect fit.

Final finishing and shaping calls for great skill and is done with plane, draw-knife and spokeshave. Perfect shape and balance is the ultimate goal, with some bats being balanced to the requirements of individual players. After sanding and burnishing, and with the handle bound, the final stage is to brand the cricket bat with the maker's name and grading stamps. Who dared mention aluminium?

The craft of the bat maker echoes the timelessness of England's traditional summer sport: cricket on the village green has changed little since 1850.

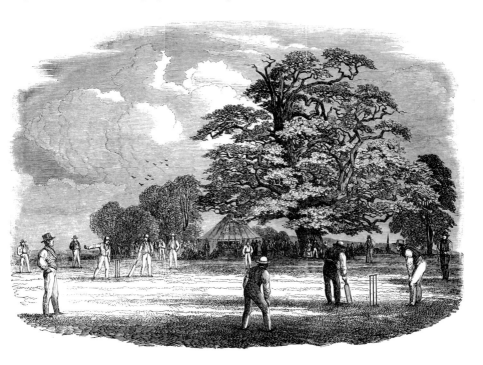

Game and Gamekeepers

PHIL DRABBLE

The keepers I grew up with killed anything with canine teeth or hooked bills. Hawks and owls, badgers and hedgehogs, foxes, stoats and weasels were all on their little list. So were carrion crows and magpies, jays, jackdaws and rooks – they were on the blacker-than-black list because, rightly or wrongly, keepers believed they were responsible for killing game or stealing eggs. On the grey list, the not-quite-so-bad list, were the creatures that competed with game for food or ate the food the keepers supplied before the game did. This included anything from sparrows to water hens and pigeons. They would all stop a charge of shot when the opportunity presented itself, though the keeper might not actually waste time trapping them.

Although rats were probably the worst of all the enemies of game, I never saw a rat on our local keeper's gibbet, probably because he caught them as a matter of course and thought them not worth making a song about. Stray dogs were liquidated and buried discreetly because the English are sentimental about dogs and it was considered bad public relations to knock off Man's Best Friend, but there were no such inhibitions about cats. Every keeper worth his salt had a row of variegated moggies' tails to decorate his gibbet, and anyone who objected was told to keep their thieving brutes at home.

Laws have since been passed to limit some of the slaughter, although keepers can (and some still do) set illegal gintraps in the secret fastnesses of their beats where officers of the law have small chance of catching them. The changing economic climate has had far more effect. Between the wars one great estate after another was broken up by death duties, farms were sold off to the tenants and literally thousands of gamekeepers were laid off.

The effect that this had on predators was dramatic. The stretch of countryside where I live covers from Needwood Forest to Cannock Chase, almost twenty miles across as the crow flies, and the whole area was once controlled by a handful of landowners. It was not socially acceptable in those days to be uninterested in sport and, since keepers' wages were between a pound and thirty shillings a week, creatures with hooked bills or canine teeth stood little chance of survival. Trying to escape from one estate to the next was simply jumping out of the frying pan into the fire.

The depression in the thirties, however, meant that the new owners, mainly smallish farmers, were far too busy trying to keep their financial heads above water to bother about what they regarded as a rich man's sport. So badgers and barn owls and their persecuted kind thrived as they had never done since firearms became fashionable.

But the predators are, after all, only one aspect of life in the countryside, however detrimental sport, especially shooting, may have been to them. The rich mosaic of woods and spinneys and copses that make English scenery so much lovelier than more flamboyant foreign parts would have been far poorer without the incentive of sport.

To have a good day's fox hunting, it is necessary to provide refuges for the foxes to lie up where hounds can find them, and other havens to which they will try to escape. It became fashionable for landowners to commemorate the highlights of their lives by planting new game or fox coverts, each a few acres in extent. Jubilee Covert, Silver Wedding Wood and similar conceits still appear on Ordnance Survey maps. Hillsides were planted with vivid banks of rhododendrons, from which pheasants could be driven across the intervening valleys, and waste land was planted with gorse to harbour foxes.

All this was good for sport, and even better for the wide variety of small birds, nesting there in safety from their natural predators which had been annihilated in the interests of pheasants.

For a while, between the wars, there flourished the best of both worlds. The variegated patchwork of the countryside was as lovely as ever before and the absence of keepers allowed persecuted species to recover. When I was at school, in Worcestershire, our Natural History Society had the run of Randan woods, unchivvied by keepers, and we were delighted by hawks and owls, woodpeckers and red-backed shrikes, badgers and stoats and hedgehogs – and still a few pheasants despite the pressures of returning predators and of locals who had no need to look over their shoulder to see where the keeper was.

It was not long before the honeymoon was over. Other things being equal, thugs will thrive over the inoffensive in most societies. Magpies and carrion crows, rats and foxes increased at the expense of lesser fry; but now the pendulum is swinging again. One of the results of the affluent society is that a new social stratum has arrived, desirous of apeing the old aristocracy by enjoying the pastimes of 'the good old days'. Instead of vast tracts of countryside being controlled by a handful of great landowners, syndicates of businessmen now rent the shooting rights from the owners of the land. Gamekeepers appear on company books as 'security officers', and other expenses can often be written off against tax if it can be claimed that giving foreign visitors the facilities of a day's shooting encourages them to pay for exports.

Shooting is now Big Business, with members of syndicates paying £1000 or £1500 apiece for the privilege of shooting hand-reared pheasants in large quantities and dressing up in gear which would not have looked out of place on the landowners and squires of the last century.

The snag is that a great many of the new shooters do not possess the expertise and love of the countryside that their predecessors acquired through being bred and brought up as part of an estate that was their family's heritage. The new men have made a pile of brass in industry, and are accustomed to evaluating both their work and their leisure in terms of hard cash. If they employ a keeper, they expect him to produce enough surplus pheasants to pay for his wages and as much of the overheads as possible. It is common practice to pay a financial incentive to keepers when the day's or season's bag of game exceeds what has been negotiated as a fair norm. A keeper rearing a couple of thousand birds may get £100 added to his wages for every day that the combined bag shot by the syndicate exceeds, say, two hundred birds.

A Sussex shooting party (c. 1910). This print was made from a glass negative recently unearthed in a junk shop by Bernard Price. The photographer was probably Percy Lapworth of Arundel.

There are various ways in which a keeper may accomplish this. He will obviously try to place his best guns where most of the action is likely to take place, while he will put the duffers where easy birds will come – or no birds at all! It doesn't encourage him to put high, difficult, and therefore 'sporting' birds over his guns if he only gets paid for what they hit and not for what they miss. But, above all, it encourages knowledgeable keepers to be at least as ruthless with vermin – or predators – as the worst of the old-fashioned Bob the Killer school.

Many of the modern bosses only turn up at the shoot on shooting days and never walk round in spring and summer, so that they have no knowledge of other wildlife that shares the land they have rented. Many of them couldn't tell a bullfinch from a bulrush if they saw them side by side. Fortunately, however, it is never fair to generalise, for there are still some very good keepers and very good bosses around who genuinely leave the countryside richer than they found it.

This is easier than it would have been in my young days. When I grew up, pheasants were reared under the bantams or laying hens that had hatched the eggs. This was a very labour-intensive process, which would be quite uneconomic with wages and food costs as they are today. At the end of the shooting season, in February, every keeper live-trapped a large batch of hen pheasants and fed and kept them in a laying pen to produce eggs for hatching. Meanwhile he went round the local farmers' wives begging, borrowing and buying and surplus laying hens, which he added to his own flock of bantams. In April and May, the domestic hens went broody and the pheasants laid up to forty eggs apiece, which were set under the domestic broodies.

When they hatched out they were put in coops set out in rows in the rearing field, about sixteen chicks to each hen. The hen was confined to her coop but the chicks were allowed to pass through narrow slats to feed in the herbage around the coops. While their foster mothers were confined, it is obvious that they were sitting targets for any hawk or owl, stoat, weasel or fox that prowled around. A keeper had to camp out in the rearing field to guard his charges against harm and I never blamed him for being pretty trigger-happy and letting fly at almost anything that could conceivably have robbed a brood of chicks. Even when the poults were big enough to go out to the wood they were anything but safe from foxes and tawny owls, so the keeper still camped out and lit hurricane lanterns at night to deter predators.

Those days are gone. Some shoots still catch up hen pheasants at the end of the season to collect their eggs for hatching, but others buy eggs from commercial game farms, which produce them on precisely the same lines as intensively farmed poultry. The eggs are then hatched in incubators and the chicks reared under hot-air brooders. Time and motion experts have laid out the keepers' workload so that one man can rear thousands of chicks where chaps in my day could only rear hundreds. Keepers are now expected to water and feed in a couple of hours, morning and night, on some shoots and help out with general work of the farm for the rest of their time. Even when the birds are put out into the wood, they are put into fox-proof wire netting release pens, from which they are gradually allowed to wander further afield with very little need for skilled supervision.

The advantage from the conservation angle is that pheasants are now physically guarded from predators, so that the need to destroy every creature with a hooked bill or canine teeth has largely gone and keepers who still do so are pretty old-hat.

My experience is that men who live on the land they shoot over, as farmers and a few individual landowners still do, usually appreciate their heritage of wildlife and don't shoot simply for the sake of getting big bags. A nest of long-tailed tits in a clump of gorse fills their eyes with as much pleasure as a covey of partridge on their stubble. They would far rather watch a litter of badger cubs in their wood than sell the skins for shaving brushes; they appreciate their luck in being able to afford their sport and are prepared to rear a few extra pheasants for hawks and owls, instead of believing that the money they own buys them the right to exterminate anything in the countryside that might jeopardise their fun.

These men usually choose keepers who are also in tune with the broader canvas of rural ways, and they are wise enough not to put them under pressure or offer them incentives that encourage protection of game at any cost. When a keeper knows that the boss understands the technicalities of his art, notices when badger setts or tracks cease to be used, and will question the sudden disappearance of hawks or owls, his respect will be such that he is unlikely to push his luck.

Such relationships do nothing but good. Farmers who love their sport are less likely to grub out every hedgerow to grow the last hundredweight of corn. And, if they do, they will probably plant up odd corners with nesting and holding cover that is appreciated as much by small birds and mammals as it is by potential fodder in the game larder. Stubbles that are left to over-winter are as popular with flocks of linnets and yellowhammers as they are with resplendent cock pheasants. Pools that are left unfilled in field corners are tenanted by frogs and toads and newts as well as wild duck. And untidy fallen trees, beloved as cover by pheasants, also provide wood-boring beetles that attract woodpeckers. This apparently natural scenery is far more rewarding than prairie farms or regimented forests.

I number among my friends several keepers who work under this type of regime and it is always exciting to join them on their beats. They take pride in being able to pinpoint a sparrowhawk's nest in what had been a crow's nest the year before. Less conscientious men would have put a charge of shot through it 'in case it contained another clutch of crow's eggs'. The fact that hawks suffered 'accidentally' would be a matter of no consequence.

The real keepers, the chaps that I respect, don't shoot things by accident and they enjoy proving that their deeds match up to their convictions. Their skills in coping with real vermin, the rats and carrion crows and magpies, are in no way inferior to their predecessors'. In my young days, there were two standard ways of catching crows – trapping or poisoning. In trapping, an egg was surrounded with a ring of gintraps; when any animal or bird approached the egg, it put its foot on the treadle of the hidden trap as surely as if it had hit a minefield – and the result was as indiscriminate and horrific. Whether it was innocent or guilty, the steel jaws gripped and shattered the bone in its leg with equal impartiality. And there it stayed in agony until the keeper chose to come round and hit it on the head.

The alternative was to lace eggs with poison: picking up a dose of strychnine was just as certain a death, and didn't end there; the poison is so persistent that, when the victim dies, it will in turn poison whatever eats it, and that victim will poison the next customer at the corpse too.

Thanks be, modern keepers are precluded from using either gintraps or poison, though chemical pesticides spread on the land are still as bad as anything in olden days and pest officers are allowed by law to use strychnine for killing moles.

Good modern keepers take pride in more finesse. I know one who can imitate the call of a carrion crow with such fidelity that every crow in the wood will come to investigate when he lets off his throaty croaks. I have seen him sitting under the cover of a tree, nursing a .22 rifle with a silencer ('sound moderator', the gunsmiths call it now) and every crow that settles in the topmost branches of a nearby tree becomes a trophy of sheer skill instead of the luck of the poisoner. I know keepers who can 'squeak-up' foxes and stoats by sucking air through their lips in imitation of a rabbit's cries when he is caught, and magpies will come to scold a ferret tethered on a collar and line – they bite the dust as surely as the villain in any Wild Western.

But the skills of modern keepers are also similar to the skills of intensive poultry husbandry. Disease and boredom are worse enemies than any predator. When thousands of young birds are being reared in close confinement pestilence spreads like wildfire. Instead of shooting rabbits and boiling them with rice for chicken feed, as old-fashioned keepers did, their modern counterparts buy processed poultry pellets which have been liberally laced with antibiotics. The poults are reared in such close confinement that they cannot find insects so they pluck out each other's feathers to pass away the time.

Left alone this would inevitably lead to cannibalism, so the keepers trim off the tips of their beaks to prevent them closing enough to grip a feather by the tip. They can still scoop pellets from a trough but, even if an earwig ran across their feet, they'd be hard put to it to pick it up. By the time they would naturally have left the hen they are large enough to fly up to roost, and their trimmed beaks should be growing sufficiently for them to begin to forage in the wood. At this stage they are put out into large enclosures called release pens, erected in the covers from which it is eventually hoped they will fly the gauntlet over the guns. They are by then too large for possible damage from hawks or owls, and foxes are their most likely enemies. Competent keepers can cope with these without traps or poison.

In short, the harm that keepers once wreaked on a wide variety of wildlife is no longer necessary, although there are still too many men who have never got over the indoctrination of their predecessors. If they are allowed to bring shooting into disrepute, I blame nobody but their employers. A pocketful of fivers does not entitle them to exterminate everything but game in the interests of sport. If they have been too busy coining easy cash to learn respectable codes of conduct they mustn't grumble at being regarded as outsiders. The way to cut their corns is not to prosecute the man on the beat for killing protected birds or beasts but to put his master in the dock as the responsible cause of the trouble. Publicity is a powerful weapon and those who take up sport as a status symbol, to prove to the world that they have made it, don't relish hitting the headlines for unacceptable conduct. Keepers who get their bosses into such hot water soon find themselves redundant.

There are, admittedly, goodies and baddies on both sides of the fence. Between the wars, when times were hard, few keepers took it very seriously if a local poacher spent a night with a long net catching rabbits, or got a pheasant silhouetted against the moon and clobbered it with his catapult. If he got caught he'd have his long net confiscated and, if he'd got more pheasants than he needed for the family's Sunday dinner, he might well land up in court. I knew one burly fellow who could drift through the wood as silent as a shadow and who was a marvellous shot with his catapult, which he called his flirter. He never got caught with any incriminating evidence for the simple reason that he never took his spoils home with him. He hid it in a ditch and, next day, his wife took the baby for a walk and brought the booty home in the bottom of the pram!

His modern counterparts have no such skills. Some sneak round the lanes in motor cars, shooting feeding birds with rifles and making off before there is time to catch up with them. Since pheasants now cost several pounds apiece to rear and are often as tame as domestic poultry there is little difference between poaching them along the roadside and stealing a barnyard hen.

88

Phil Drabble and Angela Rippon choosing a ferret at the Game Fair. With patient handling these traditional working partners of gamekeepers and poachers can become interesting and lively pets.

But the worst menace that modern keepers have to cope with are the thugs who come out from the towns. A very professional keeper from a great estate grumbled bitterly to me because his boss had agreed to have the annual Game Fair on his land. He didn't mind the crowds or the hullabaloo from the clay pigeon shoot or the litter that he knew would be left behind. What worried him was the gangs of hooligans from a city about twenty miles away who would pay to come to the fair, not to see the exhibits but to make an accurate plan of the coverts on the estate so that they could return later in the season and plunder the pheasants.

Although likely to be outnumbered, good keepers are not easily outwitted. The man in question arranged a demonstration of 'keepers' dogs' as one of the main attractions of the fair. A typical keeper with neat plus-fours was seen patrolling along the river bank where the fishing display was staged. He had an exceptionally fierce-looking Alsatian at his heels. Another man, in the guise of a suspected poacher, moved from one clump of cover to the next on the far bank. (It was no coincidence that his clothing was made of heavily padded leather.) Meanwhile a commentator gave a vivid description of the keeper's duties over the public address system. When the interest of the crowd was thoroughly aroused, the keeper spied the poacher and roared out a challenge across the river. The 'poacher' gave the expected insolent reply and the dog was told to get him. Without a second's hesitation, the great dog plunged into the water, swam across and gave chase, pulling the 'poacher' down and dragging him, screaming, to the bank. Heaving him into the river, the dog dragged him across and brought him back to the keeper, who arrested him. It was a very impressive demonstration which can have done little to inspire prospective poachers on that estate with confidence. They were not to know that the whole thing was a hoax. The dog was a highly trained police dog whose handler was in mufti, simply dressed as a keeper.

Such exercises are by no means all bluff. Modern keepers have to be equipped with modern equipment. They use walkie-talkies so that they can spread out at night until they pinpoint the intruders and call up reinforcements before tackling them. Many of them use the latest light-intensifier binoculars, which were developed on the battlefield for soldiers to spot the enemy without giving away their position by showing a light. These binoculars can literally see in the dark and, although they cost around £1000 apiece, soon recoup their cost by saving birds which might otherwise have been stolen by the hundred.

Gamekeeping is now a sophisticated, scientific business in which very large sums of money are often at stake. Responsible sportsmen do the countryside and wildlife far more good than harm. A few exceptions sometimes bring their fellows into disrepute, but the effective way to deal with them is to publicise their actions so that they are ostracised by respectable folk.

The Gunmaker

BERNARD PRICE

An old single-barrelled gun hangs upon my wall, the barrel made of twisted steel, the fore-end and stock of well-figured walnut. The hammer perches at the side like a vigilant bird, and the under-lever flows back under the trigger guard in a line that is the very essence of good design. It is not a grand presentation gun, rich in engraved ornament and chasing, but a simple workaday gun and the steel butt-plate is worn sharp from more than a hundred years of hard use. I purchased the weapon twenty years ago from an elderly gamekeeper about to retire. When I took it to my local gunmaker to have it checked for safety, I was astonished to find that he recognised the nipple of the striker as a replacement he had made years before.

Such is the craft of the gunmaker; he builds guns for the individual, and takes a personal interest in their care for as long as he lives. London-made guns are renowned throughout the world and have been so since Charles I established the Gunmaker's Company of London with a charter in 1637. Soon after the custom developed of testing guns by loading and firing them with charges well beyond normal usage and then carefully examining them for flaws; so it was that Viewing and Proof Marks came into being, and they are as dependable as the Hall Marks on English silver.

During the sixteenth century the value of the gun for hunting game became established, although most of the shots taken would have been aimed at 'sitters'. Shooting for sport began to take root in Britain on the Restoration of Charles II in 1660; he had acquired a taste for it while living in exile in France. By the eighteenth century the sport was widespread, and the country squire with his dogs and fowling-piece became a familiar image of the day. It was a period that saw the making of superb flintlock weapons. Many of them were at first fitted with barrels from Italy or Spain, but by about 1750 the London makers were producing excellent gun barrels of their own. The tubes were fashioned from quantities of horseshoe nails which were heated and worked

91

The stocker's tools. Note the rack of gauges and bottoming tools and the needle files on the right. The stock has been made and fitted, and left rough.

into solid strips of metal, then wound around a mandril, fire-welded and hammered into a barrel. Many improvements were made to guns over the next century, but the most important was the development of the breech-loader following its appearance at the Great Exhibition of 1851. As with many good ideas it was strongly opposed, but the new breech action eventually won popular acclaim. No longer would the sportsman suffer 'a flash in the pan' when at the fall of the flint the priming powder failed to ignite the muzzle-loaded main charge.

Many of the old guns were mounted with silver or gold. Decoration in the form of silver wire was frequently let into the stocks, and the lock-plates provided a perfect opportunity for the skilled engraver to work his scenes of the chase. Such names as John and Joseph Manton, W. Greener, John Twigg, James Purdey, Griffin, Delaney, Boss and a score of others are as renowned in gunmaking as the names of Chippendale, Hepplewhite and Gillow are in furniture design and cabinet-making.

Today the old craftsmanship has been combined with modern technology, enabling the finest gun barrels to be made from original solid forgings and bored straight for all barrel sizes and weights. Guns are made to the specification of the customer, to fit his size and suit his strength more exactly than a hand-made silk shirt. To purchase a pair of such guns requires a deep purse, for they can cost several thousands of pounds. The desire of the wealthy shot to own the best guns he can afford is the key to the continuing success of the gunmaker, and there is no shortage of apprentices ready and capable of following the gunmaker's art. From the lumps of rough walnut and rust-covered barrel blanks, a work of art emerges as well as a fine gun. Master craftsmen lap out the bore of the barrels to create correct choke sizes that will throw perfect shot patterns at forty yards. The great names of British gun-making sign their weapons with far more than their name, and there is no better guarantee to the purchaser.

John Bakall alters the bend and cast-off of a gun. After pouring boiling linseed oil over the grip he applies pressure to push the stock over.

On the Banks of Loch Lomond

TOM WEIR

Loch Lomond was in brilliant show-off mood for the *In the Country* team that September day when BBC cameras were trained on Angela Rippon setting off with ornithologist Roger Lovegrove into the yellow reed beds of the river Endrick marshes to look for plants and birds, while Gordon Beningfield and I started our climb above them, up the narrow edge of Conic Hill which is the very crest of the Highland Boundary Fault.

I had met the team for the first time over dinner the previous evening, and in the course of our chat had talked about the very special capriciousness of Loch Lomond in manufacturing its own weather, producing wild squalls of wind and rain in one part while another can be serenely biding its time, earning a reputation among sailing men of being a really wicked old lady. Now she was smiling, and Gordon and I were happy to be moving briskly on a chilly morning of rainbow colours on hill and loch, as the sun played hide and seek with the fast-moving clouds – there was never a dull moment. As yet our view was relatively limited, but the joy of Conic Hill is suddenly clearing the trees, mounting steeply, and in an instant seeing it all there.

'Look at that!' Gordon exclaimed, a look of incredulity on his face. 'Yes,' I said, 'you're standing on the exact dividing line between the Lowlands and the Highlands, and if you cast your eye down you'll see how our ridge goes into the loch and rises over the crest of one island after another. The nearest one is Inchcailloch, then Torrinch, and beyond it Creinch, with a gap, then the biggest island on Loch Lomond, Inchmurrin.'

Gordon chuckled. 'A lot of inches. You haven't gone metric yet on Loch Lomond.' 'No,' I said. 'Because big as Loch Lomond is, the biggest surface area of fresh water in Scotland, its glory can be measured in inches, the islands. The word "inch" comes from the Gaelic "innis" meaning an island. Look at that lot just to the north of us, forming a real archipelago as the hills northward rise more steeply. The loch is shallowest where it is broadest, from the

94

Endrick mouth through the maze of the main islands, marvellous for sailing. Notice though how the big triangular base, nearly five miles broad, contracts as if shut in as the peaks get higher. Well, the loch is ten times deeper up there, a plunge to no less than 600 feet below Ben Lomond. The story of the varying depth of Loch Lomond and its sudden broadening as it goes south is in the rocks. In the north the mountains are of hard Highland schist and the glaciers of 10,000 years ago had to dig deep to force a passage. But when they encountered the softer rocks of the Highland Boundary Fault they could push them aside. The islands are the gritty masses which withstood the ice.'

It was then that Gordon let me into a guilty secret. He had never in his life visited any island. Why? Because he doesn't like boats. I felt we had to put this right, since Inchcailloch is only a few minutes' passage from Balmaha, and down there waiting for us was Alex MacFarlane whose forebears had been boatmen on Loch Lomond for over 250 years.

'Aye, I hope they'll bury me over on Inchcailloch wi' the other robbers,' grins Alex, whose first visit to the island was when he was carried over in his mother's arms as a baby when she walked across the frozen strait from Balmaha. It was a nice wee heave across the water to the island, choppier than I expected, and I could see that Gordon was glad to have broken his record with such a quick landfall. One step from the boat and he was among the splendid oaks once harvested for their bark for tanning, but abandoned to nature in the nineteenth century.

Inchcailloch was purchased by the Nature Conservancy Council in 1962 because of the glory of its semi-natural oakwoods. The Nature Conservancy Council welcomes visitors and provides a Nature Trail pamphlet which fully explains the points of interest along two and a half miles of path, whose crowning viewpoint at 250 feet is reached by sleeper walkway, laid with loving care and leading to a welcome seat. With over 20,000 visitors to the island each year the sleeper trail became necessary because the natural path was eroding.

I have seen the value of good management here. In the days before 1962 there was none, and you couldn't get near the ancient burial ground for the tangle of brambles. Now it is a grassy meadow, and you can read the clan names of MacFarlanes and McGregors on the weathered stones.

The church foundation, 64 feet by 19 feet, and dating to 1225 or earlier, was built to honour St Kentigerna 300 years after her death. St Kentigerna was the mother of St Fillan and daughter of the King of Leinster. She retired to this Loch Lomond island at the end of her life, dying here in A.D. 763. Inchcailloch, meaning 'island of the old women', refers to the nuns who were probably followers of the Saint and kept her memory alive. Following these early days of colonisation of Scottish islands by missionaries of the Celtic church, the religious orders had the right to exploit the Loch Lomond woods.

Logs were also taken across the loch and down the river Leven in the fifteenth century for shipbuilding at Dumbarton.

After this Inchcailloch seems to have been cleared of its timber for farming, until the demand for oak bark for the tanning industry resulted in a great planting of oak for coppicing. The system was to divide the wood into 24 sections called 'hags' and crop them on a 24-year rotation, one hag being cut every year. This is the way to get a maximum crop of bark, for the stumps of the felled trees begin growing again immediately, putting out new shoots which are thinned for better production. By the year 1800 the coppicing system seems to have been well established on Inchcailloch and regular cargoes were being sailed from Loch Lomond to the Glasgow and Greenock tanneries.

When we arrived Angela and Roger were already on the island with Senior Warden John Mitchell. He was explaining the succession of events, showing them the ruins of the farm buildings whose lease was not renewed after 1770, and the veteran oaks, with their massive trunks and wide-spread limbs, which had escaped coppicing and were left to grow as seed providers. Like us, they were enchanted by the semi-natural forest which resulted when man abandoned coppice management and left nature to go its own way. True, the oaks are narrower and less expansive than those which had been seed providers,

The paddle steamer Maid of the Loch *passing through the narrows at Balmaha on the wilder east side of Loch Lomond. Beyond are the oaks of Inchcailloch nature reserve.*

Alex MacFarlane delivered mail to the Loch Lomond islands for more than twenty-five years. The natural beauty of the area which he worked so hard to preserve is now threatened by the plan to build a pumped storage electricity system on the Loch.

but it is as close as we can get to a natural oakwood, with an exceptionally high density of birds including pied flycatcher and two kinds of woodpeckers, green and greater spotted. The arrival of the spring migrants is a joyous time, when the woods ring with the songs of willow and wood warblers, while buzzards mew and redstarts jangle.

Going back in the boat Angela and Roger enthused about the variety of their morning, the marshes and the shallow pools with flighting duck, herons, reed buntings, whooper swans, greylag geese – they had even seen a peregrine. To be upsides with them we told them of our fast-flying merlin which had curved across the sky on pointed wings.

Boatman Alex MacFarlane eased the engine to keep the spray down and leaned across to point out the island of Inchfad behind us. 'In my great-grand-father's time, about 1783, he had a distillery over there; none of your illicit stuff, though there used to be plenty of that. Duncan his son was a shoe-maker at Balmaha, and the Excise appointed him to collect the whisky tax before the spirit was sent away from the loch doon the Leven. You were talking aboot the oakwoods. My grandfather used to take birchwood to the Paisley Mills – they used it to make bobbins for the thread. He had a scow and sailed it from where the wood was cut right to the mills, following the river Cart up from the Clyde. Then he'd fill up wi' coal and get pulled up the Leven wi' trace horses to get back into Loch Lomond.'

In our original plan Angela and Roger were to go off with Alex and cruise westward round some of the other islands, including Inchgalbraith where the osprey used to nest on the castle ruins. But the rising waves and the vicious wind which had arisen suggested a change of plan. And a good thing too, for when Gordon and I drove north for Rowardennan we heard that several canoes had been turned over in a squall.

Winding along in the car from the Pass of Balmaha I was telling Gordon what magic this side of the loch had always had for me, a gateway to the wilds in my teenage days when I worked in Glasgow. On Saturday nights a group of us would catch the last bus after a hard day working in the shops, and at 10.30 p.m. shoulder our rucksacks for the six road miles to Rowardennan. Then we were on a grassy footpath leading us to our promised land, the wild Craigroyston shore, where at around two o'clock in the morning we would unroll our sleeping bags under an overhanging rock on a grass shelf above the burn, feeling like Rob Roy himself.

Yes, that was the life. Below us the oakwoods plunging to the shore, bluebells and primroses everywhere, the rowans in blossom; above us the Cuilness gorge which splits the wild side of Ben Lomond, a stronghold of pied flycatchers, red deer and wild goats. Down across the loch is Inveruglas Castle, sacked by Cromwell's force. As Gordon and I climbed up the gorge we could look across to the passes on the west side of the loch, by the Lairig Arnan and the Dubh Eas, cattle-droving routes which brought easy pickings for the McGregors and the MacFarlanes, whose lawless ways persisted long after they had died down elsewhere. At Inversnaid the Government built a barracks to contain the McGregor clan, but Rob Roy waited for it to be finished before he swept down and destroyed it.

As I ended my spiel, Gordon suddenly burst into song, intoning in a voice as unmusical as my own 'For ye'll tak' the high road, and I'll tak' the low road, And I'll be in Scotland afore ye.' I had then to answer his question, 'Which road are we on, anyway?' – the fact that we were both alive and well meant we were not on the Low Road, which refers to the route taken by a dead spirit back to the place of its birth. The song is said to have been written by a man from Balmaha district, waiting in Carlisle jail for the death sentence to be carried out. He wrote the words of the song for the sweetheart whom he would never see again, and entrusted delivery to a friend who was taking the High Road of life back to his home.

'Let's see what the Forestry Commission has done on this side of the loch. We'll take a walk along the shore past the Commission's camp site at Cashel for a look at something I know will interest you.' So out we went on a narrowing point to the Cashel itself, which is the Irish word for a ring fort or Christian establishment. The drystone wall encircles an area of about 90 feet by 80 feet, and could date from as far back as the sixth century, to the time of St Kessog who built a monastery on Inchtavannoch near Luss across the loch.

From here we looked across to Inchlonaig, noted for its big scattering of yew trees, descendants of those planted by Robert the Bruce to equip his bowmen for Bannockburn, it is said. In the mid-seventeenth century this island became a deer park belonging to the Colquhouns of Luss, and there is a sad story of an event which took place just over a hundred years ago, when Sir James Colquhoun, fourth Baronet, went over to shoot fallow deer with his keepers. They were to provide Christmas venison for the people of Luss village. At the end of the day the boat was seen passing Inchconnachan only a mile from home, but neither the boat nor its occupants were ever seen again.

A few steps southward along the point was something it would be easy to overlook – a flat pile of stones far enough out on the water to be difficult to reach. But if you know where to search, you can find the submerged causeway leading out to the stones, which are the remains of a crannog, a lake dwelling. For security against intruders its unknown builders made an artificial island 80 feet by 60 feet, carrying a house, and possibly a stockade for their animals. Crannogs continued to be used into the Middle Ages, it is thought.

Now for a walk on the Sallochy Forest Trail, a mile up the road and climbing into the Rowardennan Forest. This is part of Queen Elizabeth Forest Park, which extends beyond the slopes of Ben Lomond and right over its top into the Trossachs, an area which has been protected by a National Parks Direction Order since the late 1940s. No National Park as such was ever set up in Scotland but in 1953, to commemorate the Coronation of Her Majesty, much of this great area was designated the Queen Elizabeth Forest Park, with the principal purpose of timber production and a secondary one of increasing recreational opportunities for walking on the hills and enjoying the shore. Among the dense stands of spruces above us I knew we would get shelter, and with luck a good view from the top, if the clouds enveloping the hills broke open.

The grassy ribbon of path climbs swiftly, past an old 'bloomery', a hearth where in pre-industrial times the oaks were burned to make charcoal for smelting iron from the iron ore which was brought to Sallochy bay. In those days the whole eastern shore of the loch from Balmaha right to Inversnaid was being intensively worked for oak bark, charcoal timber and 50–60 year old logs which were mature enough for naval shipbuilding. Estate books reveal a big labour force, and the children helped strip the bark, traditionally done between 1 May and 10 July, when it peeled easily. The new shoots on the stumps then had time to grow before the onset of winter.

There was even an acid works at Balmaha, which used the oak after it had been stripped of its bark. Cut into six-feet lengths and heated in cylinders, the stripped wood yielded a coloured liquid which, when distilled, produced pyroligneous acid from which vinegar was manufactured as well as creosote and dye. Even the coppice thinnings were used to make hoops for barrels, while from the ash trees cart wheels and handles for spades were made.

The Forestry Commission trees of today are grown for a quicker return. The spruces and larches are planted in blanket fashion, but some oak and birch have been left to give variety and colour. Through an edge of cypress we swung left into gloom, then found ourselves in a rectangular clearing of farm ruins. An explanatory notice board with an outline plan of the buildings told us that two hundred years ago this had been a clachan of five families, working the land jointly. Its name was Wester Sallochy, Gaelic for a wet or boggy place. On this high shelf above the steep drop to the loch its people would have raised cattle, some taking them to the high pasture in summer, while others got on with the job of working the infield and outfield to produce as much food as they could for themselves and their livestock. At that time, nine out of ten people in Scotland worked on the land. No doubt they would have had the simplest of diets, oatmeal and milk products mostly. From their sheep would have come the wool to make their clothes.

Gordon was interested in the way nature has taken over the old walls, putting living green amongst the stones where ferns sprouted with thistles and nettles. A Scots pine had taken hold on a wall as though in protest at all these foreign spruce trees encroaching. While Gordon dug out his sketchbook and seated himself to make a drawing, I had a close look at the main farm building, taken over eventually by a single family who had added mortar and built two gable-end fireplaces, one of them ornamented with a mantelpiece of pink sandstone. Slates had replaced thatch for its roof. I found it hard to believe that this place was still being farmed at the time when I left school.

Gordon held out his sketchbook for me to inspect. He had drawn a section of thick drystone wall being submerged by feathery ferns and moss, symbolising dead stones and living nature – the life force that eventually obliterates the sins of man, though it may take a very long time, as we could appreciate having gone back over a thousand years of history in a morning on Inchcailloch and Strathcashel Point.

But what of the future? Man in the past progressed slowly. Now in the nuclear age he moves fast and can plunder any natural resource at such frightening speed that the decision-making process becomes ever more crucial when big issues are at stake, such as the plan to build the biggest pumped storage electricity scheme in Europe up there on Ben Lomond. What would it involve? First, a widening of the twisting road to Rowardennan along which Gordon and I had driven singing about 'the steep steep side of Ben Lomond'. The road would keep on climbing right up to 1600 feet, to a hollow across which would be built a huge sloping-wall dam. And into the Craigroyston shore of the mountain a power house chamber would be dug and a tunnel driven so that water could be pumped out of Loch Lomond into the big hollow, which would become a reservoir.

This mighty and costly piece of environmental destruction would produce of itself no electricity. The power to pump the water from Loch Lomond 1600 feet uphill would have to be bought in at off-peak price. The profit comes when the water is brought down through the generators producing power that is sold at a higher price at times of peak demand. Pumped storage is a support system for thermal or nuclear power stations with a steady output. It provides a means of supplying extra power when it is needed. The first phase of the Ben Lomond Scheme would take ten years to build and would store and regenerate 1600 megawatts. But we already have a conventional power scheme immediately across Loch Lomond from Ben Lomond. It is called Loch Sloy after its high reservoir. In the early 1970s the intention of the North of Scotland Hydro-electric Board was to convert this to pumped storage and provide all the capacity we needed up here. Why do we not have a converted Loch Sloy instead of the proposed new Ben Lomond Scheme which would mean two hydro-electric schemes facing each other across Scotland's finest loch?

Talking about this with Gordon as he finished his sketch by the ruins of the two hundred year old homesteads we wondered what the clachan folk would make of the modern lifestyle in which we enjoy standards of luxurious comfort, leisure and entertainment they could never have dreamed of. We attribute it to the industrial revolution, to the mastery of technology fuelled by the resources of coal, oil, electricity, gas and nuclear power. But more and more thinking people are voicing doubts about the road along which technology is leading us, wondering if we should not be taking less from the environment instead of more. I see Loch Lomond as symbolic of the dilemma facing us in the future. Here we have a natural world of outstanding beauty, exceptionally rich in wildlife, within easy reach of three-quarters of the population of Scotland, between the Clyde and the Forth.

By the happy accident of its ruggedness, the Craigroyston shore has remained free from development, and today could be called an outdoor lovers' paradise, recognised as such by the sensible Committee who set down priorities for National Parks in Scotland. Their solid work produced the protection order which safeguarded Ben Lomond and the Craigroyston shore now under threat. Breach that wilderness with engineering works and pylons and something irreplaceable has gone for ever.

In economic terms the loch performs an invaluable service as the main reservoir of Central Scotland, providing 100,000,000 gallons of water per day for domestic and industrial use. Since the early 1970s a barrage on the river Leven has controlled the outflow of Loch Lomond with the objective of maintaining a level 26 feet above Ordnance Datum. Luckily the National Nature Reserve was well established when the conversion from natural loch to reservoir was undertaken and so the interests of man and nature were considered at every step, or we might have lost the shore margins and many of the little bays. Over thirty species of waders have been recorded in one small portion that could easily have been inundated and the feeding ground lost.

Environmentally I think that the 1970s produced a good balance on Loch Lomond between conservation and development. The Forestry Commission has done much to accommodate tourists, providing them with picnic spots and even barbecue spots near sizeable car parks. Forest walks and nature trail pamphlets guide visitors towards enjoyment and respect for the loch, while backpackers and naturalists have a wealth of adventurous tracks and secret places, from the marshes to the heights where the alpine plants bloom high in the corries. In the micro chip age, when we all have more leisure, we are going to need the spiritual renewal of Loch Lomond even more than we did in the past. I sensed that my visitors knew that too; I hoped they would return.

Tom Weir and his contemporaries were the 'first generation of working class outdoor folk' and for people who follow in their footsteps Loch Lomond is still a source of inspiration.

Autumn on the banks of Loch Lomond. Looking west to Inchfad.

Gordon Bening field sketching the magic of Loch Lomond from the vantage point of Conic Hill – right on the line of the Highland Boundary Fault.

The Sawyer

BERNARD PRICE

Sawyers worked in pairs, as much a team as a pair of plough horses, but I doubt if they were ever as happy. George Sturt said he never knew a sawyer smile. The sawyer's task was formidable: it was to urge the trunk of some great tree over the saw-pit and then to saw it into planks from end to end.

The top sawyer was the man in charge, but neither he nor his mate below would have been men of any great intellect – if they were they could not have done the job, year in and year out. They needed above all brute strength. It should not, however, be thought that they were men without craft. They understood raw timber; the problems of a curving trunk; the need for an excellent pit-saw, sharpened, set, and maintained at the peak of condition. It was a method of sawing timber that continued virtually unchanged from medieval times until well into the twentieth century.

Using iron timber-dogs, the trunk of some great elm would be levered over the pit, to rest on wooden rollers straddling the deep trench. The sawyers marked the line of their cut with a length of twine and chalk or charcoal. The bottom sawyer would then settle himself in the gloom of the pit. The top sawyer, having already checked the saw and the line of the cut, looked next to the angle of the blade, and when all was ready the hours of laborious sawing began. Both men would sweat, but the bottom sawyer had the sawdust to contend with too. A lapse in concentration and the top sawyer could ruin a tree by going off line by an inch; a stroke at the wrong angle and the saw would jam. Occasionally the two men would stop while the bottom sawyer oiled the blade. Cuts for several planks would be made, until the first roller was reached. The bottom saw handle was then unfastened, and the saw removed from the trunk so that the rollers could be moved forward. The saw was then replaced again, and the labour continued. When the planks began to vibrate in the trunk they would be fastened with ropes and steadied with wedges. An undiscovered nail in the timber would bring

Country boys watching work in one of the last surviving sawpits. The tree trunk rested on rollers over the sawpit. When the sawyers reached the first roller, they had to remove the saw and roll the next section of trunk over the pit before work could proceed.

exasperation and oaths, and half wreck the teeth of the saw. While the top sawyer set about his repairs in unpaid-for time, his mate probably adjourned thankfully to the local pub and would not have hurried back.

Such men cut the planks and timbers for the buildings of Britain, the furniture, the wagons, the ships and the coffins. They measured their lives by the rasping metronome of the quarter-inch saw cut, a race of men who vanished overnight with the coming of the steam-driven saw.

Nature Writers —
A Personal Choice

BERNARD PRICE

The recognition of the individual voice of truth emerging in any facet of art is always a personal discovery of rare delight, and particularly so in literature. It requires no orchestra, set stage or gallery for appreciation, simply the complete quiescence of the mind of the reader. There are many and various definitions of what does or does not constitute Art, but I believe the term may be applied to all those things which cause the imagination to react, work and communicate. Such qualities know no barriers of time; the writings of Gilbert White, for example, are as fresh and full of meaning now as when they were first published in 1788.

The task of the nature writer is one of the most difficult of all and yet, with poetry, it is probably among the most frequently attempted, often with disastrous results. The writers responsible are seldom aware of their deficiencies, finding it impossible to understand why their sentimental descriptions of animal and bird behaviour and their hackneyed portrayal of landscape should give the discerning reader cause to reject such embarrassing outpourings. It is the writer who brings to his subject the truth of knowledge and understanding, born out of close personal observation and told with the clear voice of plain language, who rings a whole carillon of bells through the spirit.

Spirit is not too strong a word, for the romanticism and the worship of nature that so rapidly developed in England during the early eighteenth century was to sweep Europe like a new religion. William Collins and Thomas Gray wrote poems that sound like a chorus of hymns, while James Thomson's 'The Seasons' introduced a degree of realism as well as of sentiment in its treatment of nature. Wordsworth was to declaim:

> One impulse from a vernal wood
> May teach you more of man,
> Of moral evil and of good,
> Than all the sages can.

Wordsworth and other writers of the day discovered mysticism in the countryside, particularly among forest, hills and mountains. They lived in humble country cottages and regarded walking as a spiritual activity rather than a necessity brought about by the lack of suitable transport. For many of us, walking in the countryside continues to be a source of relaxation and inspiration; the changes taking place in our lifestyle and leisure pursuits in this final quarter of the twentieth century do nothing to devalue this basic yet civilised joy. For three centuries most of the great country writers have also been great walkers. As Leslie Stephen wrote in *In Praise of Walking*: 'I have fancied myself on such occasions a felicitous blend of poet and saint – which is an agreeable sensation. What I wish to point out, however, is that the sensation is confined to the walker.' Or as George Macaulay Trevelyan so magnificently made the point in his famous essay 'Walking':

> I have two doctors, my left leg and my right. When a body and mind are out of gear (and these twin parts of me live at such close quarters that the one always catches melancholy from the other) I know that I have only to call in my doctors and I shall be well again ... I never knew a man go for an honest day's walk, for whatever distance, great or small, his pair of compasses could measure out in the time, and not have his reward in the repossession of his own soul.

Today it is commonplace to hear of people setting out to climb mountains and cross oceans or deserts in order to 'find themselves'; the old country writers did it all in a day's walk.

While there is undoubtedly today a great popular interest in the countryside and its creatures, the interest is by no means generally well informed. As Edward Thomas commented more than seventy years ago, 'Enthusiasm without knowledge is not enthusiasm.' We have tended to move away from the low-key comment and warmth of the old writers in favour of coffee-table books and tales of organised adventure exploited by advertising and public relations. If the population of Great Britain were to be canvassed I wonder what percentage of its fifty or so million would be found to have read Gilbert White's classic *The Natural History and Antiquities of Selborne*. I was astonished to discover recently that three broadcasters of my acquaintance, two of whom have contributed programmes on the countryside, were totally ignorant as to the identities of Gilbert White and Richard Jefferies.

It was the great quest for an understanding of nature that drove John Constable and J. M. W. Turner, both countrymen, to paint as they did. Both men were in love with light and wedded to the realistic fulfilment of their observation, as can be seen in Constable's *Hay Wain* and Turner's *Country Blacksmith Disputing upon the Price of Iron*.

Detail from James Thomson's 'The Seasons', first published 1726–30.

Although in early childhood I lived in a house on the edge of a market town surrounded by rich countryside, we had few books at home and my reading on country matters was mainly confined to the newspaper articles of John Armitage and Frances Pitt. When aunts and uncles came to know of my interest it was not long before I began receiving books as gifts, particularly those by W. P. Westall.

At the age of eleven I entered a new world. The school lending library was not a great room, merely a large brown-painted cupboard with two doors opening like wings. Inside were some fifty or sixty volumes, and the first book I borrowed was *The Gamekeeper at Home* by Richard Jefferies. That book transformed my outlook on the countryside, and a year later I met the seventy-five year old gamekeeper of a nearby small estate, who schooled me in his craft and on the country generally whenever I had free time over the next six years.

I read every book by Jefferies that I could lay my hands on. He must stand among the greatest nature writers of the Victorian era, although during the past fifty years there has been some criticism of his writing, and it is true that he does at times build effects by simply cataloguing natural images and sounds. Thomas Hardy uses a similar device in his descriptions of the lanes of Dorset, but they relate more to the human experience because of the stories into which such descriptions are set. Hardy and Jefferies met briefly in 1880.

Richard Jefferies was born in 1848 at Coate Farm near Swindon. In about 1866 he began work as a journalist on the staff of the *North Wilts Herald* and spent twelve years doing newspaper work and attempting to write novels in his gabled bedroom. He seems to have received considerable encouragement from his editor, and in 1872 he wrote a letter of several thousand words to *The Times* about the labourers of Wiltshire. The letter was printed in full, with the inevitable result that he was immediately hailed as an authority on agriculture. Five years later he moved to Sydenham in order to be nearer the London editors. When *The Gamekeeper at Home* was published, first as a series of articles in the *Pall Mall Gazette* and then in book form, he was firmly acclaimed as a writer of note, and some even spoke of him in the same breath as White of Selborne. Books followed fast: *Wild Life in a Southern County, The Amateur Poacher, Wood Magic, Round about a Great Estate, Nature in London, Red Deer, The Open Air* – all are in similar vein, with their great feeling for nature and their sympathetic sketches of country people.

Jefferies' sentences are neatly turned and evocative; this one is typical of his style: 'Green rushes, long and thick, standing up above the edge of the ditch, told the hour of the year as distinctly as the shadows on the dial the hour of the day.' He did not write only natural history books. There was also *Bevis, the Story of a Boy*, and, at the end of his desperately short life, the novel *Amaryllis at the Fair* which he dictated to his wife, being too weak to work with a pen. It is in *The Story of my Heart*, however, that he fully reveals his religious passion for the countryside and for life. The words spill from him like his breath – for six years he suffered from tuberculosis of the lungs and the intestines. His final home was at Goring, in Sussex, and it was there that he died in the August of 1887. He was buried in Broadwater Cemetery where, thirty-five years later, the body of another naturalist, W. H. Hudson, was also laid to rest. Many years ago I planted young holly bushes on their graves, plants that I had taken from a plantation W. B. Yeats had known, but neither of them survived.

William Henry Hudson was born in Argentina in 1841, growing up to appreciate all creatures from mammals to insects. He collected for the Smithsonian Institute and wrote on the ornithology of Buenos Aires, and in 1870 was elected a corresponding member of the Zoological Society of London. In May 1874, Hudson arrived in England and began a remarkable career as a nature writer. Although he had a home in London it was the south-west of England that became his particular field of study. His curiosity was insatiable, and whatever excited him also fired his compulsion to pass on his enjoyment through his writings. In this he was highly successful, although, like Jefferies, his financial rewards were meagre to say the least. His best known books are probably *The Naturalist in La Plata, Idle Days in Patagonia, Birds in a Village, Birds in London, Nature in Downland, A Shepherd's Life*, and *Far Away and Long Ago*.

Although he considered himself field naturalist before writer, his writing is none the less of the very first order. Wiltshire, with its vast open spaces, reminded Hudson of his early South American home, and he developed a feeling for the country, as he describes so well in *A Shepherd's Life*:

> ... it is the likenesses that hold me, the spirit of the place, one which is not a desert with the desert's melancholy or sense of desolation, but inhabited, although thinly, and by humble-minded men whose work and dwellings are unobtrusive. The final effect of this wide green space with signs of human life and labour in it, and sight of animals – sheep and cattle – at various distances, is that we are not aliens here, or invaders on the earth, living in it but apart, perhaps hating and spoiling it, but with the other animals are children of Nature, like them living and seeking our subsistence under her sky, familiar with her sun and wind and rain.

Hudson spent most of each year walking the countryside and, while his own scholarship was considerable, he tended to be impatient with the naturalist who drew nourishment only from books. He disliked what he termed 'indoor society' for it bred an 'indoor mind', the intellect that saw insects as pests, while Hudson loved them. His knowledge of Hampshire insects was probably unrivalled during his lifetime. Hudson also had an ear for the rustic voice such as the Somerset lad he describes, who worked as a bird scarer and said of swifts: 'They screechers be curious birds. Did you ever hear, zur, that they be up flying about all night and come back in the morning?' His description of the boy is reminiscent of the hand of Dickens:

> He was a singular-looking boy, about fourteen to fifteen years old; very thin, with long legs, small head, and sharp round face, and was dressed in earth coloured, threadbare clothes much too small for him. With that small

sharp face and those shifty eyes under his little grey cap, he looked curiously like some furred creature, a rat or vole, with perhaps dash of stoat in his composition, and if his nose had been longer I might have added that there was even a touch of the shrew-mouse in his appearance.

One of my most treasured books is the first edition of *Birds in a Village*, Hudson's first essays on bird life in England. It is an important book which made many people aware for the first time of the beauty and usefulness of birds. He drew attention to the senseless killing of birds by fruit farmers, in the same way that many fish farmers today are indiscriminately killing herons and kingfishers. He exposed fully the market in exotic plumage from other countries, and confessed that he would rather see larks eaten than placed in cages. W. H. Hudson was totally unafraid of vested interests where wildlife was concerned, and reputations did not deter him either; more than once he challenged Darwin as to the validity of statements in *The Origin of Species*.

Still among the best-loved of the English literary naturalists, however, is Gilbert White, who wrote a century and more before Jefferies and Hudson. My first introduction to the work of Gilbert White was from a schoolmaster who had recognised my interest in the countryside, and the first copy of *The Natural History of Selborne* that I ever owned was the Penguin edition, published in March 1941. Looking back, I often reflect on the importance and sheer boldness of republishing the book at that time; there, in the midst of the darkest maelstrom of war, was floated a gentle life-raft of sanity.

Throughout the eighteenth and nineteenth centuries the clergymen of country parishes found time to compile works of local history and topography, lists of flora and notes on archaeological discovery. Such a bequest has proved a more than bountiful gift to the twentieth century; no doubt they were all stimulated by White, and later many of them were to be shocked by Darwin.

Gilbert White was born in Selborne in 1720. He was educated at Oxford, held several curacies, became curate of Faringdon, the neighbouring parish to Selborne, in 1755 and in 1784 was appointed to Selborne, where he remained as curate until his death in 1793. His writings extend to over a hundred thousand words but the most important and most popular are the letters regarding life and natural observation that he wrote to his friends Thomas Pennant and Daines Barrington. There are more than 150 English editions of the book and it has been translated into many languages. While making a programme for *In the Country* during 1979 I met a young Japanese man who, his eyes glowing with enthusiasm, showed me his Japanese copy of White. He was even more delighted when I told him that I had known Edmund Blunden, who had edited that particular edition.

Another of my friends was Anthony Rye, whose remains now lie buried in Selborne churchyard where he walked so often. Rye's book *Gilbert White and his Selborne* (1970) really is the best introduction one can have to White the man. The book begins: 'He was a little, thin, prim, upright man, and used to go poking about in the lanes and hedges with his stick ...' Yet this eccentric old curate, with his eagle eye and remarkable knack for interpreting what he saw, has succeeded in making himself and his village celebrated throughout the world. He discovered new species, in some ways anticipating Darwin, but it is his way of writing and his reflection of a total, detailed environment that is so enchanting. He surprises us with such observations as: 'My musical friend remarks that many of his owls hoot in B flat; but that one went almost half a note below A. The pipe he tried their notes by was a common half-crown pitch-pipe, such as masters use for the tuning of harpsichords; it was the common London pitch.' There are many lovely villages in Britain, but it is at Selborne that Gilbert White has left the benediction of his voice and footprints over and upon the landscape, a Shangri-la where the curate lives on for ever.

So many country writers have enhanced our appreciation of landscape and nature, and those I recall here are writers for whom I have particular regard. High among these ranks William Cobbett. Born in 1763, he came from Farnham in Surrey where his father was an innkeeper and farmer. To me Cobbett is the very image of what I regard as the old yeoman farmer. He began work in the fields soon after he could walk, scaring birds and weeding wheat. Before he reached his teens he could reap and drive a plough team – his father said the boy worked as hard as any man in the parish. At the age of nineteen he had his first sight of the sea from the top of Portsdown Hill, and he said then that it spoilt him for being a farmer. Cobbett led a colourful life: he was imprisoned twice, travelled to America, and became bankrupt in 1820. But it is for the perceptive journalism of his *Rural Rides* that we shall remember him, and for such comments as: 'There is no pleasure in travelling, except on horseback or on foot. Carriages take your body from place to place, and if you merely want to be conveyed they are very good; but they enable you to see and to know nothing at all of the country.'

George Borrow is another writer to whom I turn at least once a year, for the colour, legend and travel that permeate his *Lavengro* and *Romany Rye*. Another great walker, Borrow sang as he walked all over Britain and in many parts of Europe, while children would shout after him 'gipsy' or 'witch' because of his strange appearance. He was not interested in natural history; for him the countryside was the open air, travellers, the elements, and the sheer physical joy of dealing with them.

I find myself charmed repeatedly by country diarists and so are many others, judging from the success of the television programmes that dramatised the jottings of Francis Kilvert. But what of Parson Woodforde and all the lesser-known keepers of journals? To glean among their great crop of words is enough to sustain and entertain a reader through any hard winter.

As railways spread and linked their branches about Britain, so writers from the city began to venture into the countryside. It provided them with much new material, and the weekend rambler was born. Harriet Martineau wrote her *Guide to the English Lakes* and urged townspeople to come and visit. The books of Wilkie Collins were among the first ever to be sold on railway bookstalls, and he too prospected for rustic plots whenever his train stopped unexpectedly at some country station, returning as quickly as possible to the safety of the city in order to write them. The Georgian poets at the turn of the century also indulged themselves in dalliance with rural England, although it was a little like gardening in a dinner jacket and far removed from the sweat-stained shirt of John Clare. Even so the modern voice in poetry that was to explore the imagery of the countryside in such exciting fashion was not far away. Robert Frost, Edward Thomas and W. H. Davies vigorously signposted new paths. Once again they all walked, even though 'super-tramp' Davies had a wooden leg as the result of a railway accident in America. On one occasion, when on his way to visit Edward Thomas, Davies slipped and broke his wooden leg while climbing a hill. He stayed with Thomas while the local wheelwright made a new one; it was fashioned using measurements and a drawing because Davies did not want it to be known that it was a wooden leg. When the wheelwright brought the leg to the house he described it on his bill as a novelty cricket bat, price 7s. 6d. Edward Thomas is my favourite poet of the English countryside, and I am always grateful for having known and talked long with his widow, Helen, who told me much about him during the final weeks of her life.

I have covered many a long road with the ballads of Hilaire Belloc running through my head, and in many a pub or tent a volume of H. J. Massingham or Brian Vesey-FitzGerald has given me pleasure and instruction before I settled down to sleep. It is, however, Henry Williamson whom I regard as the finest prose writer of countryside and nature in this century. We met many times, in Devon, Hampshire, Sussex, Bristol and London. He was not an easy man to know, but if you were fortunate to be his friend he abounded in generous good humour and splendid conversation. His creative urge burned deep into his final years. I once found him exhausted, after two days and nights of writing without food or sleep. He is famous for *Tarka the Otter*, indeed his face always reminded me of an otter; but there are so many more books, such delights as *Dandelion Days*, *The Dark Lantern*, *Tales of a Devon Village*, some forty books in all. Henry Williamson remains the master of English descriptive writing, born of a life in symphony with the natural world.

Saving Our Bacon?

JOE HENSON

There are many breeds of farm animals which were once commonly seen populating our fields and hillsides but are now so rare that some are in danger of becoming extinct. I am often asked if the reason for this was some lack of hardiness or disease resistance, or a degeneration in their own ability to provide the food products for which they were kept. My answer must be quite the reverse. As their numbers declined only the best and most efficient individuals were retained. Where breeds were isolated geographically, like the Soay sheep of St Kilda or the Orkney sheep of North Ronaldsay, they had to fend for themselves and only the fittest and most thrifty survived. Why then did they decline? The answer is partly economic and partly fashion.

The standardised breeds of cattle, sheep, pigs and poultry which were developed in the eighteenth and nineteenth centuries and lasted up until the 1930s were capable of fulfilling several roles. Cattle were bred as draught animals which were then eaten at the end of their working life, while the cows produced milk for the family and butter and cheese for sale. Sheep were developed for their wool and were only eaten as mutton after producing several lambs and fleeces. They were also milked and many of our most famous cheeses were originally made with sheep's milk. Lowland flocks were folded on roots which were followed by wheat. The 'golden hoof' was the only way of providing fertility on lowland farms before the days of artificial fertilisers. Dung was second in value only to wool, and to kill lambs at three months of age, as we do today, would have been unthinkable. Herds of pigs were used to reclaim rough ground in preparation for crops, or herded through the forests to live on acorns, beech mast and fungi; they were later fattened on household scraps and other waste food. Poultry was selected for the courage of the cockerels, as the prize fighters were worth large sums to sporting gentlemen for their cock pits. The hens were chosen by natural selection for their mothering ability; the best broodies reared the largest number of chicks to live on and breed again. At the end of its laying life, a plump hen was destined for the pot.

Joe Henson feeding his Gloucester Old Spot pigs. Hardy and prolific, they were the ideal cottager's pig; today they suit the smallholder more than the intensive commercial producer.

Our popular breeds of today have been selected for quite different reasons. After the industrial revolution, when our population changed from being rural to largely urban, the few people left in the countryside had to feed the hungry town-dwellers. They had to produce more food per acre of land and per head of livestock. Maximum production linked with show-ring breed standards became the criteria of selective breeding. Heavy-milking black and white dairy cows took over when motorised transport, pasturisation and chilling enabled the remotest dairy farms to supply fresh milk to distant towns. The show ring decreed that they should not be red and white or have the black colouring of their legs touching the hoof – hardly important factors for yielding milk. The quantity of concentrates they were fed was not taken into account in the milk production competitions entered by breeders; nor were hardiness and thrift, or the ability to live and produce on sparse grazing and cheap fodder considered. Cows were bred to be efficient specialists: to produce the maximum volume of milk regardless of cost of production or quality of product. The result today is over-production of low-fat milk at too high a cost.

Similarly our beef breeders started with big rangy draught animals but, as families became smaller, the market required a small joint. The beef bulls in demand for export to North and South America were also required to be of a small early-maturing type to reduce the size of their range cattle. Today the demand is more for lean, tailored, supermarket beef, produced from grass as cereals are now too dear to feed to cattle. This requires large lean ranging cattle maturing at a much greater size. To satisfy quickly the new demand for larger breeding stock breeders went to the continent, where many diseases are endemic, to bring back the big breeds which are still used for ploughing. For ploughing muscle is needed and muscle is lean meat. Had they continued to develop native breeds like the Longhorn and the South Devon they would not have had to import cattle with the associated disease risks.

These days our sheep breeds have been bred to produce one thing, fat lambs. With the ever-increasing cost of land and labour the milk-fed fat baby lamb is becoming a luxury product. We can no longer afford to copy New Zealand, where land and labour are still cheap and grass grows for eleven months of the year. The most expensive part of producing a lamb in this country is getting it born. After that surely it makes sense to let it grow to mature mutton and produce a fleece. But we are told that, with the invention of synthetic fibres, wool is no longer in demand; and mutton comes from old half-dead ewes, so nobody wants it. I wonder if that is really what the consumer demands, or only what she is told she wants. I know what I like my socks to be made of, and it's not nylon.

Today's pigs are tailor-made for lean bacon. Many are born in farrowing crates under infra-red lamps and never see the daylight or feel the mud beneath their snouts. Britain's pig industry, in trying to compete with that of the Danes whose land is even scarcer and dearer than ours, has been snared into an intensive system with an upward spiral of costs. Having built the buildings and installed the automatic lighting, heating, ventilation and meal-feeding system and employed a pigman who is acually a computer programmer, how do you cut costs when inflation does not include the cost of the product? You can't turn all those factory-bred pigs out into scrub land to root for a living – they would not earn you one. All you can do is spread your overheads by packing more pigs into the same building, and may the Lord forgive you.

We are told that battery hens are the most efficient converters of cereals into consumable protein that we have. In order to produce the maximum number of eggs per year, broodiness has been bred out of them; incubators and electric brooders are so much more efficient when you are hatching and rearing thousands per week. Also, thanks to the broiler chicken industry with its fast-growing table chicken, we don't need to eat the pathetic hens when they have finished their enforced stint of egg laying.

So what of the livestock industry of tomorrow? Do we breed even more highly productive stock dependent on costly feeds, packed even more tightly into our controlled-environment houses and stuffed with more antibiotics to ward off diseases against which they have no natural immunity? If so, do we allow our historic breeds of livestock, unable to adapt to this 'Star Wars' system of husbandry, to die out and be lost for ever? I don't think we can afford to. Luckily, enough farmers and conservationists in the early 1970s thought the same way. They formed a working party which resulted in the foundation of the Rare Breeds Survival Trust whose job is to ensure the survival of the unique combinations of genes held in our rare breeds of farm livestock.

In the past, changes in farming systems which have led to breeds being phased out of commercial use have happened gradually over the years. This time-lag has enabled breeders to redirect their breeding policy and select from within their breeds for factors to suit the changing fashion. As the world gets smaller, with rapid improvements in communication and transport, our market requirements are controlled by world trade rather than local demand. World trade in turn is often affected by political decisions which can be taken overnight. OPEC doubles the price of oil and intensively housed livestock ceases to be profitable. Russia makes it up with the United States and buys all its surplus grain; the price of grain doubles and livestock breeds dependent on a cereal diet are no longer viable. Farmworkers are awarded a massive rise and many shepherds are priced out of a job; sheep breeds requiring intensive management have to give way to primitive breeds which can breed and survive without constant supervision.

Although dairy products are overproduced in the Common Market, we are still importing butter from New Zealand. Our dairy herds are concentrating on the liquid 'doorstep' market which requires a low-fat milk. Suppose we suddenly fell out with our Continental neighbours and withdrew from the European Community, and at the same time New Zealand formed a trade alliance with Japan and stopped supplying us. Suddenly we would have to produce our own butter, cheese and milk powder and our dairy farmers would be paid for quality rather than quantity. Breeds capable of producing high-fat milk like the Jersey and Guernsey would again take their rightful place at the head of dairy cow society and even cheese-producing breeds with high-protein milk like the Old Gloucester might be welcomed back into the club.

The possible combinations of political whim and climatic disaster are endless, and yet there are still people who claim that there are too many breeds of livestock in their country and that the breeds in current favour are the only ones that should be allowed to survive. How short-sighted can they get? I implore the countries of the world to nurture their local minority breeds as a valuable national asset. We must maintain a broad base of domestic genetic material from which our livestock breeders of the future can choose. Each breed contains a unique combination of genes and once a breed is lost it is gone for ever, never to be recovered.

Old Timers for the Future

Polled British White Cattle

The origins of the Polled British White cattle are lost in antiquity. One theory is that they were brought to our eastern shores by the Vikings, and this is supported by the fact that an almost identical breed called the Fjallras is still in existence in Sweden today. They were once a popular dual-purpose breed in the eastern counties but, like all our dual-purpose breeds, fell from popularity and are now rare.

The cows were good milkers, often yielding 1000 gallons per lactation, and the steers grew fast and produced a high-quality lean carcase. The fact that they are naturally hornless and transmit this to their progeny if crossed with a horned breed is a useful attribute. In the past they were exported to hot countries, where their white coat and dark pigmented skin protects them from sun and heat. They have attractive black points – ears, eyes, nose, feet and teats – and, while the black around their eyes protects them from the glare of the sun, their black noses and teats are less susceptible to sunburn. This probably explains why there are more Polled British Whites in South America than there are in Britain today.

I predict more British White bulls being used on the heifers of our hardy hill beef breeds for easy calving and to produce milky hornless suckler cows.

Dexter Cattle

In the late nineteenth century a cattle breeder in Southern Ireland by the name of Mr Dexter noticed that the local breed of Kerry cattle were producing a percentage of miniature calves. He gathered these together and established the diminutive breed bearing his name. They became popular with the local small peasant farmers, as they were cheap to keep and thrived on sparse grazing and poor-quality roughage. Being small they were more easily tethered and milked by the women while the men were away wage earning.

These convenient little cattle, which milked well for their small size and also fattened readily, were soon exported to England, where they rapidly gained popularity with smallholders. A breed society was formed in the year 1900. In the depression between the world wars, many smallholders were forced out of agriculture and their farms were amalgamated with larger holdings; their numbers dropped dramatically and their little cattle became rare.

Once a rare breed, Dexter cattle are now in great demand. Their size and milk yield make them popular on small farms and with seekers of the self-sufficient 'good life'.

After the war, few of the remaining Dexters were bred pure as there was no market for their tiny calves. Breeders requiring more milk crossed them with Jerseys and if beef calves were wanted an Angus bull was used.

Today the pendulum has swung, as it so often does. There is an enormous demand for small farms, and self-sufficiency and an escape to the 'good life' is all the rage. Pure-bred Dexters which fit the smallholder's bill are wanted so urgently that breeders cannot breed them fast enough to meet the demand.

Gloucester Old Spot Pig

Once known as the orchard pig, as it was often kept in the orchards of the Berkeley Vale near Gloucester to live on the windfall apples, the Old Spot was the ideal cottager's pig. Besides being hardy and prolific, Old Spots were also a very docile breed, making them ideal mothers. They were able to fatten on household scraps and waste food, a valuable asset for the smallholder.

In the nineteenth century, when the breed was developed, there was a demand for animal fat, since vegetable oils were not then available. The Old Spot satisfied this need admirably as it readily laid on fat and would be kept until it had reached a gross size. Nowadays, however, we require a long lean pig to produce lean bacon in intensive conditions. Excess fat became a dis-advantage and the Gloucester never took to very intensive management, so it became a rare breed.

But if it is kept out of doors, grazing and living on roots and natural foods with plenty of exercise, surplus fat need not be a problem. If our commercial pig producers ever decide to return to a low-cost system of outdoor pig-keeping they could not do better than to base their breeding on the Gloucester Old Spot.

Cotswold Sheep

When the Romans colonised the south-eastern quarter of Britain, they brought with them a long-woolled type of sheep to produce the wool necessary to keep them warm in our inclement climate. All our long-woolled breeds of today are descended from these Roman sheep, and are found in counties south-east of the Fosse Way which marks the border of the area most inten-sively settled by the Romans.

An important member of this family of breeds was the Cotswold, which gave the name to the area where it was kept: *Cottes*, sheep folds, *Wolds*, bare hills. Throughout the Middle Ages wool was the most important product of this country and almost its only export, and the Cotswold sheep played a major role in this industry.

The Cotswold was also a good producer of lean mature mutton, and a leg of mutton eaten hot on Sunday lasted cold for the rest of the week. I believe that if fat baby lamb is priced beyond the housewife's purse, she will want to learn how to cook delicious quality mutton bought at a price she can afford. The signs are already evident that there is a returning demand for wool and I can see the big, long-woolled mutton breeds like the Cotswold being called upon to play a leading role in our sheep industry again.

Soay Sheep

The Soay is the oldest known breed of domestic sheep in the northern hemisphere and is thought to have been kept by Neolithic man in Stone Age times. The last remnants of the breed survived by being isolated on the Island of Soay in the St Kilda group, where they remain pure to the present day. All the Soay sheep in Britain now are descended from sheep brought back from St Kilda.

The Soay has survived unshepherded for centuries and is therefore ideal for nature reserves needing a small, light-grazing animal to balance the ecology in an area requiring the minimum of human disturbance. Unlike most com-mercial sheep they are naturally short-tailed and keep their hairy britching wool clean, rarely attracting fly strike. Each year they shed their wool naturally

Joe Henson with his collection of rare breeds of sheep – a Soay is in the foreground.

and it can be gathered from the thorn bushes as in ancient times. Both sexes are horned and the rams will help the ewes keep marauding dogs and foxes away from new-born lambs – a thing I have never seen in any other breed. Most important of all, they are completely immune from foot rot, making the shepherd redundant apart from the compulsory annual dipping.

Dorking Poultry

A Roman writer who died in A.D. 47 described poultry of the Dorking type with five toes, but no one knows whether these birds were brought by the Romans or were found here on their arrival. Either way their ancestry certainly dates back to Roman Britain.

Dorkings typify the old utility barnyard chickens which formed the back-bone of the poultry industry before the age of the intensive poultry specialists. They are short in the leg which helps prevent damage to their large eggs, as the hens tend to lay standing up in the nest. They are excellent broodies, being able to cover a large brood of chicks, ducklings or even goslings, and have strong mothering instincts. The capons make delicious, heavy, roasting birds if you are tired of tasteless broilers and the hens provide a plump boiling fowl for an old-fashioned chicken stew at the end of their laying life.

The Dorking comes in five colour varieties – silver-grey, red, cuckoo, dark and white – all of which would grace the backyard of anyone wishing to convert their household scraps and tail corn into meat and eggs.

The Victorian Farmworker

BERNARD PRICE

The men who work on the land have always been Britain's most undervalued asset. Once regarded as mere peasantry, they were promised from the pulpit that the meek would inherit the earth. They never did, but they fought and died for it from Agincourt to Alamein.

Victorian art tended to view the rural scene through rose-tinted spectacles, following the example of the painter George Morland who, fifty years earlier, had depicted an idealised rural life. Ragged but charming children held open farm gates, ostlers pulled their forelocks, milkmaids smiled prettily as they carried heavy pails over broad fields, while shepherds and their flocks were particularly popular as symbols of Christian belief, and china shepherds and shepherdesses decorated the mantelpieces of the gentry. The privileged were as far removed from the life of the Victorian farmworker as is the tractor driver of today, listening to Radio One in the comparative comfort of his cab.

The Victorian farmworker was a man who needed above all to be physically strong and the master of many skills. The best of them could sink a well, lay a hedge or thatch a rick as well as carry out the multitude of daily tasks required through the seasons on a farm. They exulted in their expertise with tools, planting and animal husbandry.

Such men believed in self-help, and rabbits were often taken home to help fill the pot. Most gamekeepers were highly suspicious of them, and not without reason, for opportunities of taking other creatures besides rabbits were many. A catapult was a deadly weapon in the hands of a man who had used one from boyhood. Mushrooms were obviously collected and many a clutch of pheasant eggs would have been cracked craftily into a milk can and carried home to provide nourishment for a young family. Watercress, nuts and black-berries were all to be obtained in season, and if an enterprising farmworker lived near a town there would be a market for ferns, bulrushes and moss for window displays to bring in a few extra shillings. Such activities were also the province of the gypsy and the moucher but, while the farmworker respected their knowledge and cunning in the countryside, he considered himself superior, enjoying the daily discipline of regular work.

A degree of high living such as I have described depended entirely upon the area in which the farmworker lived and upon his employer. During the middle years of the nineteenth century a labourer might well have been paid only seven or eight shillings a week, which was totally inadequate for maintaining a family. This was sadly reflected in the quality of their food. Potatoes were undoubtedly the staple diet, probably eaten year in and year out for breakfast, lunch and supper. Bread was baked at home but there would have been little butter. Tea was rarely to be had when it cost eight shillings a pound – a week's wages. The drink that most often started the day, apart from beer, was hot water poured over burnt crusts crumbled into the pot. In some parts a brew called 'salt sop' or 'tea kettle broth' was consumed; it consisted of pieces of bread and small portions of butter, lard or dripping in a basin with hot water poured over it. Bread and cheese was also a standard meal, while for the lucky ones fat pork and bacon were to be had from time to time, although meat was rare for the labourer in the countryside. When meat was available it was usually offal and made to last for as many days as possible.

Pause for refreshment – probably cider – with haymaking in full swing. Neither the men nor the horses rested for long until the crop was safely ricked.

For the majority of Victorian farmworkers it was as though Lent lasted all year, and any variation in the staple diet was long remembered. No wonder Christmas became such a welcome feast in the nineteenth century. When the potato crop failed, turnips, cabbages and barley meal only partially filled the gap. A Select Committee report in 1867 stated that the most under-fed counties were Cheshire, Dorset, Kent, Rutland, Shropshire and Staffordshire; seven years later North Devon was added to the list. Even when a cottager was able to own and fatten a pig, he could not always eat it; extra money at harvest time might pay the rent of the cottage, but the price of the pig might be needed to clothe the family. In Wiltshire the workhouse diet was judged better than that received at home by half the men in work.

For farmworkers in many parts of the country, therefore, the provision of food and a rainproof roof must have been of constant concern. Improvements to cottages and the design of new ones became a subject of wide interest; Prince Albert himself designed some. In time better cottages, with reasonable sanitation, fireplaces, and windows that actually opened, began to be built, but during the first two decades of the present century there were still many farm cottages which left much to be desired. In 1902, Anna Lee Merritt described the labourers' cottages in the now fashionable village of Hurstbourne Tarrant, in Hampshire, in these words:

> ... little whitened huts, curiously compounded of bricks, timber, hurdles and mortar (called expressively wattle and daub) and covered with thatch. From a distance they are scarcely distinguishable from the ricks. Two or three tiny rooms shelter large families living by unceasing toil; toil which has no reward but daily bread, and hardly enough of that. And yet in this narrow home, affection and self-sacrifice find room enough.

Village communities were astonishingly insular. Farmworkers lived most of their lives on one farm, and where conditions were good they took great interest in its management; there was always rivalry between such farms in doing their work just a little better than each other.

In summer they began work at 6.00 a.m., and finished at 6.00 p.m.; during the winter the hours were from dawn to dusk. It was not common in the Victorian era for farmworkers to be able to read and write, but that does not mean that they were in any way lacking in common sense or humour. I have always believed that it is far easier for men, working together, to face and contend with hardship than it is for their wives, who are so often isolated for much of each day. It would be wrong to say that farmworkers did not lead isolated lives, for they frequently did. Old men have told me how they would 'talk to themselves' when working alone. They did not mean that they were talking aloud, it was simply their way of describing meditation and thought. I know of hurdle makers who rarely saw another person during long periods of work in the coppice, leaving and arriving home in darkness. These men always appeared to be happy, and had a highly developed instinct for the understanding of human nature and the recognition of individual character.

The one link with the outside world was the country carrier, who would circulate with horse and cart between the villages and the nearest town in any given area. I was fortunate in knowing several of these before they began to vanish from the scene some thirty years ago. All of them were characters and greatly respected among the rural communities they served. Harry Chase once told me this story about Bill Sharpe, who was a carrier between Arundel and Havant. When the parcel post came into service it dealt a severe blow to the country carriers. Once, when passing a churchyard where a funeral was taking place, Bill noticed that some of the bearers were postmen, then a spare-time job. 'Ah,' called Bill, 'another poor bugger gone off by parcel post!' Such rough but quick and perceptive humour still abounds in the countryside today.

The fact that the labour of many more men was required on the Victorian farm, in comparison with present-day requirements was not entirely due to the lack of machinery and the different farming methods. The average diet of most of them made a long day with a high work rate almost impossible. It also enabled illness to obtain an easy foothold, and infant mortality was considerable. Today we hear very little of tuberculosis, scarlet fever, diphtheria or typhoid, but all were rampant in the nineteenth century. Cholera was not at all uncommon and was usually spread by a contaminated water supply, due either to the seepage of sewage or to the contamination of wells by surface water. The village of Pyecombe, for example, renowned among all shepherds and those with an interest in country matters as being the home of a famous style of shepherds' hook, suffered a cholera outbreak in 1849; eleven people died, but after the water supply was changed there were no further cases.

Agricultural mechanisation and the steady movement from the land has brought great change to the village as well as to the farm and the farmworker. A century ago, in an average size village, about ninety per cent of its population would have earned their living from the land. Now that figure might well be reduced to three per cent, and certainly to below five. Two dozen men equipped with scythes mowing barley in a large field a hundred years ago would have gone home in the dark with the results of their labour lying cut in the field. It would still need to be raked, carted, threshed and dressed, then some fifteen tons of barley would be ready for carting to the maltster. These days three men with a combine and two tractors might harvest a yield four times greater than their Victorian predecessors and when they sat down at supper their sixty tons of barley would already be sitting in the barn awaiting collection. Cogges Farm Museum near Witney, in Oxfordshire, provides an

Steam revolutionised the country way of life. Its power was harnessed to thresh corn and build the rick, but often the machines brought as many problems as they solved.

excellent example of the transition that was beginning to take effect between the old farming and the new at the turn of the century. There are several such farm museums up and down the country – collections of buildings, machinery and tools that bear witness to the lifestyle of the farm labourer in Victorian and Edwardian rural Britain.

In most cases the Victorian farmer endeavoured to obtain as much work as possible from his men for as little money as possible. In order to obtain jobs men were often ready to work for less than their neighbours. A working week would have been at least seventy hours and often considerably more, and yet many farmers complained that it was difficult to find men who would milk cows, as well as doing other work, without extra pay.

In the late 1870s, due to the generally depressed condition of agriculture, the relationship between farmer and farmworker became more difficult, as may be judged from the comments of this farmer writing in December 1878:

The difficulty of obtaining good men … seems to be the chief barrier to success in farming. Able, willing, and experienced men are hard to find. Frost and snow combine together to throw a great many labourers out of employment, but the best generally are kept in their places. The recent strikes in Kent and East Sussex have caused great discussions on the subject of farm labourers. Let us hope that they will lead eventually to a satisfactory understanding between masters and men. Until this is the case, can farming ever become a successful business? What is the lowering of rents and wages? A mere reduction probably of a few pounds and shillings, which can hardly prove of sufficient moment to affect the losses in farming, or turn the scale for struggling farmers. What we want is a fair day's work for a fair day's wages, and a perfect understanding between employer and employed. When this takes place, perhaps the foundation to prosperous farming will be laid, and we may then look to Nature to favour us with better seasons. I wish I was able to make a fair comparison of the merits of the agricultural working class in the North of England, with those in the South. From what I have seen, however, wages are higher and men less experienced in the South. Their physique also suffers in like proportion. In Yorkshire, the ploughmen are out with their horses from seven till five. Here they seldom commence work till 7.30, and leave off at four. This, coupled with a higher rate of wages (to say nothing about work performed) is equivalent to a loss of at least five shillings per week per man!

None of this was the fault of the poor farm labourer, but there was more to come, as Sydney Smith showed when he wrote on the crisis in agriculture:

The responsibility of the farmers to pay a sufficient wage may sit very lightly upon them; with just half the price for their wheat which their predecessors received half a century ago, they pay quite double the wages for raising it, and more than double what is given by the foreign competitors they have to meet in their own markets. This too, they have to do, when the Legislature has relieved the peasant of every tax on the necessaries of life, and greatly reduced the cost of living. The proposed reduction in the wages the farmer has to pay, does not amount to one tenth of the fall in the price of the produce he has to sell; a ruinous cheapness the full benefit of which the labourer receives at his employer's expense.

I find the words of both writers frightening in their contempt for the work and conditions of the Victorian labouring man.

Over the years I have gathered together my own small collection of the hand tools used by the farmworkers of a century ago. All the tools are simple in design yet they will only give of their best in experienced hands and such skills are not easily won. They are tools made to last a lifetime, and were handled with skill and pride and cared for with affection. There was truth in the old saying that you know a workman by his tools: they almost formed a natural extension to the arms of the men who used them. Now they are evocative of a countryside and way of life that has disappeared; I collect them not with any sense of nostalgia, but simply admiration.

A selection of Victorian hand tools from Bernard Price's collection. If you do not know what they were used for, you will find a key on page 196.

The first of them that came to hand was an old faghook, its tip curled over by the impact of a thousand flints struck during fagging. Unlike the sickle, which has a slender crescent blade, sometimes serrated and springing straight from the handle, the faghook is more robust and its blade steps down at right angles before swinging into the familiar crescent shape, thus keeping the knuckles well clear of the ground. Punched into the blade are the words 'Fussell, Mells'; this is the name of the renowned firm of Victorian toolmakers in Somerset who sold out to Isaac Nash of Belbroughton, in 1895.

Another name I look for on old hand tools is Moss; it is revered among the past generations who used edged tools. The Moss family were blacksmiths of Hampshire who had their forges at Bramshott, Canford and Bucks Horn Oak. Throughout the nineteenth century they made edged tools using their own secret methods of tempering steel. A Moss tool was the most prized among farmworkers, and their products fetched higher prices than the very best tools manufactured at Sheffield. Their bill hooks were superb.

In Surrey, Sussex and Hampshire few farmworkers cared to use a scythe, although it was a highly efficient implement in skilled hands and there is no

Itinerant farmworkers. These people travelled all over the south of England throughout the summer months, harvesting crops and picking fruits and hops.

doubt that mowing with a scythe was the quickest and least expensive method. The farmers believed the faghook was more popular with the men because it employed more individual labour. The stroke of the faghook as it cut into the crop knocked a good measure of grain out of the ears, and many farmers said that the workers left their wages on the ground; this was gathered up by the families of the faggers as their right of gleaning and could provide them with flour far into the winter. Harvest time was the high water mark of the itinerant farmworkers. From Surrey they moved into Sussex, sometimes on to the Isle of Wight, then back for the Farnham hop-picking. Some of the best faggers were those who had been taught as boys to fag with either hand. Fagging was back-breaking work; could it be from this that the term 'fagged out' was derived?

It was also thirsty work. At hay-making, or harvest in particular, the wooden harvest bottle, a small barrel hooped with iron and fitted with a carrying handle, was well in evidence. Harvest was the time of good living, more meals, much meat, and plenty of cider or strong beer. The men started work at daylight and as an added encouragement the farmer provided a pint of ale for the first man on the field! Gertrude Jekyll, famous as a gardener and a planner of gardens, was also a collector of customs, folklore and bygone implements of farm and household. She appears as well to have had an eye for a muscular man for, as she writes in her most excellent book *Old West Surrey* published in 1904, 'A harvest bottle when not too large or heavy, is a pleasant thing to drink from, and when a fine labouring man drinks standing, with his head thrown back and his two arms raised, the attitude is generally a strong and graceful one.'

The old harvest festivities appear to have died with the coming of machines. No longer do the men hurl their sickles or faghooks at the last sheaf on the farm, nor do they decorate the 'last load' before it is carted in triumph from the field, with the corn dolly representing the Celtic corn goddess Ceridwen, the counterpart of Ceres, held aloft.

At the Harvest Home long trestle tables would have been arranged in the great barn. Preparations and cooking would have gone on all day. Roast joints of mutton, meat pies, swedes, potatoes and turnips filled the dishes. Strong beer, a clay pipe and tobacco were laid out at each place. Once the eating of the great supper was over and the debris cleared away, came the awaited toast to the farmer from the senior farmworker. There were many such toasts given, but this is the one I like best; it tells of the unity of people working for the common good, of how things ought to be in these islands of ours:

Here's from we and our'n to you and your'n. A wishes as how you and your folk loved we and our folk as well as we and our folk loves you and your folk. For sure there never was folk as ever loved folk half as well as we and our'n love you and your'n. So there!

Farm Parks and Museums

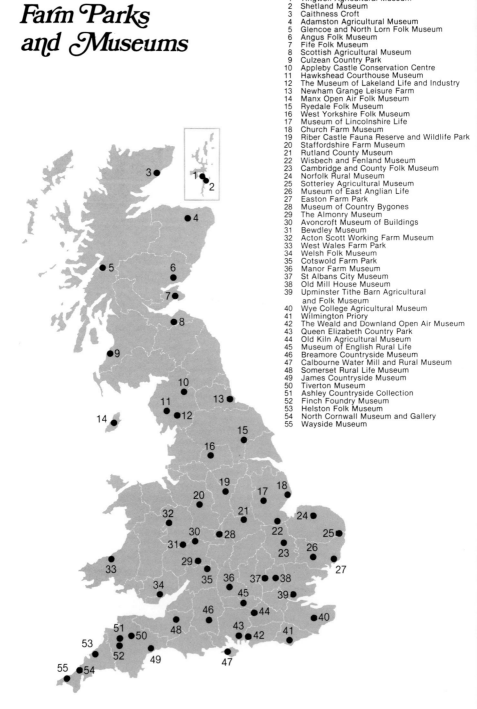

1   Tingwell Agricultural Museum
2   Shetland Museum
3   Caithness Croft
4   Adamston Agricultural Museum
5   Glencoe and North Lorn Folk Museum
6   Angus Folk Museum
7   Fife Folk Museum
8   Scottish Agricultural Museum
9   Culzean Country Park
10 Appleby Castle Conservation Centre
11 Hawkshead Courthouse Museum
12 The Museum of Lakeland Life and Industry
13 Newham Grange Leisure Farm
14 Manx Open Air Folk Museum
15 Ryedale Folk Museum
16 West Yorkshire Folk Museum
17 Museum of Lincolnshire Life
18 Church Farm Museum
19 Riber Castle Fauna Reserve and Wildlife Park
20 Staffordshire Farm Museum
21 Rutland County Museum
22 Wisbech and Fenland Museum
23 Cambridge and County Folk Museum
24 Norfolk Rural Museum
25 Sotterley Agricultural Museum
26 Museum of East Anglian Life
27 Easton Farm Park
28 Museum of Country Bygones
29 The Almonry Museum
30 Avoncroft Museum of Buildings
31 Bewdley Museum
32 Acton Scott Working Farm Museum
33 West Wales Farm Park
34 Welsh Folk Museum
35 Cotswold Farm Park
36 Manor Farm Museum
37 St Albans City Museum
38 Old Mill House Museum
39 Upminster Tithe Barn Agricultural
    and Folk Museum
40 Wye College Agricultural Museum
41 Wilmington Priory
42 The Weald and Downland Open Air Museum
43 Queen Elizabeth Country Park
44 Old Kiln Agricultural Museum
45 Museum of English Rural Life
46 Breamore Countryside Museum
47 Calbourne Water Mill and Rural Museum
48 Somerset Rural Life Museum
49 James Countryside Museum
50 Tiverton Museum
51 Ashley Countryside Collection
52 Finch Foundry Museum
53 Helston Folk Museum
54 North Cornwall Museum and Gallery
55 Wayside Museum

Gazetteer of
Farm Parks and Museums

One way of recapturing the atmosphere of country life in bygone days is by exploring the many farm parks and museums that have been opened up and down the country. They are all part of the revival of interest in the traditional ways of producing grain and vegetables and rearing stock, and represent a healthy nostalgia for those simpler times when shortage of land and energy were unforeseen problems of the future. Not that they were easy or particularly happy days for the men and women who toiled on the land – as Bernard Price has graphically described – but they were days when we still had a real contact with the soil and a true understanding of the ways of nature.

It is not surprising that the 1970s, with spiralling oil prices, prairies of mono-cultured cereals and factory farms, saw renewed enthusiasm for the methods and skills of yesterday's countrymen. Farming implements, vehicles and buildings that were rusting or rotting through neglect suddenly became collectors' items, and the start of every season saw the public début of yet another private collection thought by its owner to be worthy of wider appreciation. Other exhibits have been assembled and presented by historians and conservationists working for official organisations involved with the preservation of antiquities in their part of the country. Such collections are often run by the local authority or its museum service, but whether privately or publicly financed, they nearly all have something of interest to offer the visitor. Each of them has its own character and speciality – often based on local rural traditions. Some are only worth visiting if you find yourself in that part of the country with an hour or two to spend browsing, but others are worthy of long detours.

This gazetteer is by no means comprehensive, but it has been researched by the *In the Country* team in the hope that you will find it helpful when exploring the countryside and looking for a farm museum that is particularly interesting or well presented. There are many others and their exclusion does not mean that they have little of note to offer. Our selection is based on information available to us at the time of publication, but it would be wise if you checked on opening times before setting out to explore them.

The list is arranged geographically, and from the map you can pick those you would like to visit when in that part of the country. The main attractions of each collection have been indicated with symbols, but their absence does not necessarily mean that these features are lacking. Many of the museums are willing to make special arrangements for parties, either out of hours or even out of season. The staff that run them share your enthusiasm for the country way of life gone by.

Key to symbols

 Historic farm buildings

 Fine collection of agricultural implements

 Livestock – often rare or ancient breeds

 Agricultural workshops such as smithy and wheelwright

 A working farm – sometimes traditional and modern methods side by side

 Craft demonstrations such as saddlery and spinning

1 Tingwell Agricultural Museum

2 Veensgarth, Gott, Shetland

  Run in conjunction with a working croft, this museum is housed in a granary, stable and bothy dating from the eighteenth century. The collection includes horsedrawn implements and other tools and equipment relating to the Shetland crofter.

Open: April–September, Mondays–Fridays 10.00 a.m.–5.00 p.m., Saturdays and Sundays 12.00 a.m.–5.00 p.m.

2 Shetland Museum

Lower Hillhead, Lerwick, Shetland

  The Shetland Museum has restored a nineteenth-century croft at Dunrossness which includes a steading and watermill. The croft is complete with authentic implements and household artifacts which reflect the product of a unique cultural development closely related to Scandinavia.

Open: 1 May–31 October, daily except Mondays, 10.00 a.m.–5.00 p.m.

3 Caithness Croft

c/o Mrs E. Cameron, Laidhay, Dunbeath, Caithness

Crofts such as this were once a common feature of the Scottish rural landscape. There remain two thatched cruck constructed buildings, a long-house incorporating the dwelling, a byre and a stable, and a fine detached barn. The long-house is laid out in the style of the north of fifty years ago, and the barn houses an interesting collection of agricultural implements.

Open: Easter–4 October, daily 10.00 a.m.–6.00 p.m.

4 Adamston Agricultural Museum

Adamston, Huntly, Aberdeenshire   Drumblade 231

Most of the exhibits on display in this museum were collected from the area. They are arranged in groups including, among others, horse harness, barn machinery, butter- and cheese-making equipment and other agricultural and domestic items. Of particular interest is a hand-driven threshing mill from Glenlivet and a corn bruiser formerly used by prisoners at the Peterhead prison farm.

Open: mid-March–mid-October on Wednesdays, Saturdays and Sundays

5 Glencoe and North Lorn Folk Museum

c/o Miss B. Fairweather, Invercoe House, Glencoe, Argyll   Ballachulish 332

This museum aims to show the past life of the area. It is partly housed in two adjoining croft cottages, one being of cruck construction. The exhibits include domestic, dairy and agricultural implements, of which a foot plough (caschrom) is of particular interest. Other exhibits include costumes and tartans.

Open: mid-May–September, daily 10.00 a.m.–5.30 p.m.

6 Angus Folk Museum

Kirkwynd Cottages, Glamis, Angus, Tayside   031-226 5922

This collection, owned by the National Trust for Scotland, reflects the life of the local community and is housed in an attractive row of seventeenth-century cottages. The domestic section includes a complete period room, a dairy, a laundry and a linen weaving loom. Outside, an open shed houses a range of large agricultural implements once used in the cultivation of crops locally. The collection includes ploughs, mower reapers and also the lathe used by the Rev. Patrick Bell who made the first successful reaping machine.

Open: 1 May–30 September, daily 1.00 p.m.–6.00 p.m.

7 Fife Folk Museum

The Weigh House, Ceres, Fife   Ladybank 30410

Displayed in and around the seventeenth-century Tolbooth weigh house, this collection is fairly wide-ranging. Along with the agricultural exhibits, which include hand tools as well as larger implements, there are the tools of the clay pipe maker, reed thatcher and linen weaver. Among the items most prized by this museum is a collection of local Weaver's Society banners dating from the eighteenth and early nineteenth centuries.

Open: April–October, daily (except Tuesdays) 2.00 p.m.–5.00 p.m., Sundays 2.30 p.m.–5.30 p.m.

8 Scottish Agricultural Museum

Royal Highland Showground, Ingliston, Midlothian   Ingliston 2674

This museum covers all aspects of Scottish agriculture and countryside, both past and present. The stories are told of many items pioneered in Scotland, including James Small's swing plough, Patrick Bell's reaper and Andrew Meikle's threshing mill. The main object of this museum is to reflect the regional character of Scotland, and the exhibits are arranged to allow a clear comparison of regional variations.

Open: weekdays 9.30 a.m.–4.00 p.m.

9 Culzean Country Park

Culzean, By Maybole, Ayrshire   Kirkoswald 269

Robert Adam designed these buildings, which now house the Country Park Centre, as a farm complex. One of the rooms, the Clamjamfray, contains a collection of farm implements of chiefly the eighteenth and nineteenth centuries. Other exhibits tell the story of the estate of Culzean Castle, including that of one of the eighteenth-century tenant farmers.

Open: 1 April–31 October (The Park is open all year.)

10 Appleby Castle Conservation Centre

Appleby, Cumbria   Appleby 51402

The Conservation Centre, which is housed in the grounds of Appleby Castle, has a collection of several rare breeds of agricultural livestock, including White Park cattle, Tamworth pigs and the multi-horned Hebridean sheep. Some rare species of poultry can also be seen.

Open: Easter, 10.30 a.m.–5.00 p.m.; 3 May–30 September, 10.30 a.m.–5.00 p.m.

Harold Bettinson, the brickmaker on Peter Minter's Suffolk farm, trims clay from a simple wooden mould. Handmade bricks are now in great demand for renovating old buildings.

Gordon Beningfield and the local gamekeeper, George Bassett, wait for rabbits at the edge of a prairie field of barley. In the distance a man in a combine harvests the field on his own.

Yesterday's cornfield. Samuel Palmer's painting The Gleaning Field *(1833) recalls an era when the countryside provided a home and a livelihood – however meagre – for much of Britain's population.*

A Country Blacksmith disputing upon the Price of Iron. *John Turner's painting first exhibited in 1807 captured a rural economy that was still dependent on the working horse.*

The splendour of the working horse. Today's working breeds are more often seen on the showground or between the shafts of a brewer's dray decked with advertising.

Alan Lungley, the shepherd in Gordon Beningfield's Hertfordshire village, still uses a bilbo to restrain his sheep. The term may have originated on board Spanish fighting ships where prisoners were fettered in shackles made of steel from Bilbao.

'Smudger' Smith has worked with horses since he started farm work as a boy. Here he demonstrates the manoeuvrability of a fully laden Oxfordshire wagon.

11   Hawkshead Courthouse Museum

Hawkshead, Cumbria   Kendal 22464

The main aim of this extension to the Museum of Lakeland Life and Industry is to illustrate the range of rural occupations found, often until quite recently, in this area. The once flourishing coppice trade is of particular interest, while the agricultural basis of the area, with its predominating livestock history, is also well told.

Open: Easter, and Spring Bank Holiday–September, daily except Mondays and Thursdays, 2.00 p.m.–5.00 p.m.

12   The Museum of Lakeland Life and Industry

Abbott Hall, Kendal, Cumbria   Kendal 22464

A museum designed to help in the interpretation and understanding of the Lakeland scene, this collection tells the story of the economic and social history of the Lake District. The displays relate geology and terrain to farming techniques and practices. The exhibits include a blacksmith's forge, clog- and shoe-making as well as many interesting items connected with sheep farming.

Open: Mondays–Fridays 10.30 a.m.–5.00 p.m.; Saturdays and Sundays 2.00 p.m.–5.00 p.m.; closed Good Friday and mid-December to 2 January

13   Newham Grange Leisure Farm

Newham Way, Coulby Newham, Middlesbrough, Cleveland   Middlesbrough 316762

A working farm which is intended to illustrate aspects of the farming life of the area, both past and present. Visitors can actually see the regular life of a typical farm, while the substantive museum displays relate to its history. Many varieties of sheep and poultry can also be seen, as well as a re-creation of a nineteenth-century vet's shop.

Open: winter, Sundays 10.00 a.m.–4.00 p.m.; Easter onwards, 10.00 a.m.–6.00 p.m.

14   Manx Open Air Folk Museum

Cregneash, Isle of Man   Douglas 5522/25125

One of the buildings which make up this museum is a completely furnished crofter-fisherman's cottage. There is also a fully equipped smithy and a joiner's workshop. Weaving demonstrations are occasionally given in a reconstructed hand-weaver's workshop. It is also possible to see spinning demonstrations. A small flock of the native breed of sheep, the Manx Loghtan, is kept at the museum during the summer.

Open: mid-May–late September, weekdays 10.00 a.m.–5.00 p.m., Sundays 2.00 p.m.–5.00 p.m.

15   Ryedale Folk Museum

Hutton le Hole, York, Yorkshire   Lastingham 367
Many items reflecting the everyday life of the people of Ryedale are housed in these early eighteenth-century farm buildings. The grounds contain a display of farm wagons, machines and implements, as well as many reconstructed buildings, among which is an Elizabethan manor house, an Elizabethan glass furnace, a smithy and cruck cottages.
Open: Easter–October, daily: July and August 11.00 a.m.–7.00 p.m., other months 2.00 p.m.–6.00 p.m.

16   West Yorkshire Folk Museum

Shibden Hall, Halifax, Yorkshire   Halifax 52246
The museum is set within a fifteenth-century timber-framed house. Each room has furniture and accessories of periods which reflect almost the whole of its 500 years of occupation. A fine seventeenth-century barn contains a collection of horsedrawn vehicles, a dairy and brewhouse, and agricultural tools used in local upland farming. Around the open courtyard the farm buildings have been converted into the typical craft workshops of the clogger, the saddler, the wheelwright and others. The visitor can also see a nineteenth-century public house which was once the centre of the Halifax Luddite movement.
Open: Mondays–Saturdays 11.00 a.m.–7.00 p.m., Sundays 2.00 p.m.–5.00 p.m.; closed January and December; open Sundays only during February

17   Museum of Lincolnshire Life

Burton Road, Lincoln, Lincolnshire   Lincoln 28448
Examples of working costumes are rarely preserved, but this museum has a good collection of farmworkers' smocks and wagoners' jackets. A large collection of barn machinery and farming hand tools can also be seen, as can those of the tradesmen – such as the cobbler and saddler – who helped to make Lincolnshire villages self-sufficient communities.
Open: Mondays–Saturdays 10.00 a.m.–5.15 p.m., Sundays 2.00 p.m.–4.30 p.m.

18   Church Farm Museum

Church Road South, Skegness, Lincolnshire   Skegness 66658
This collection occupies the building and house at Church Farm. The main part of the house was built about 1760 but has been subject to mainly Victorian alterations. The interior has been refurbished to reflect the period 1900–10. Many of the items on display, including the threshing drum and mobile cornmill, were built in Lincolnshire. The barn,

cow byre and stable contain displays and exhibits illustrating nineteenth-century Lincolnshire farm life.

Open: April–August, 10.30 a.m.–5.30 p.m.

19   Riber Castle Fauna Reserve and Wildlife Park

Riber Castle, Matlock, Derbyshire   Matlock 2073
A number of rare breeds of farm animals, including sheep, pigs, goats and cattle, as well as various breeds of poultry can be seen, as can displays of old agricultural machinery and farm carts.

Open 10.00 a.m.–5.00 p.m.

20   Staffordshire Farm Museum

Shugborough Park Farm, Shugborough, Stafford   Little Haywood 881388
First and foremost this is a working farm. The predominantly nine-teenth-century farm buildings are typical of their period and geographi-cal location, and include a water-driven cornmill. Formal displays and working demonstrations illustrate the techniques of farm husbandry in Staffordshire from the last century onwards. The museum is at present the largest breeder of Tamworth pigs. These, along with a number of other rare breeds of cattle, sheep, goats, poultry and ducks, make up the livestock of the farm. The understanding and development of these once important breeds are major aims of this living museum.

Open: late March–early October, Saturdays and Sundays only, 2.00 p.m.–5.00 p.m.

21   Rutland County Museum

Catmos Street, Oakham, Leicestershire   Oakham 3654
This large collection, housed in an eighteenth-century riding school, is designed to reflect life in the former county of Rutland during the nine-teenth and early twentieth centuries. Apart from the displays of farm implements and craft tools there is a dairy section, and the larger pieces of agricultural machinery and wagons are set out in the courtyard.

Open: Tuesdays–Saturdays 10.00 a.m.–5.00 p.m., Sundays (April–October) 2.00 p.m.–5.00 p.m.

22   Wisbech and Fenland Museum

Museum Square, Wisbech, Cambridgeshire   Wisbech 3817
A general museum and art gallery which contains many agricultural items reflecting Fenland life in times past. These items include drainage tools and eel spears, but of particular interest are the tools peculiar to the growing and processing of woad.

Open: Tuesdays–Saturdays, April–September, 10.00 a.m.–5.00 p.m.; October–March 10.00 a.m.–4.00 p.m.

23 Cambridge and County Folk Museum

2–3 Castle Street, Cambridge, Cambridgeshire   *Cambridge 55159*
This museum is housed in a building which dates from the sixteenth century. The exhibits are gathered from throughout the county. The displays reflect the work and history of the people of Cambridgeshire and include the implements and tools of the thatcher, the brickmaker and the shepherd as well as those used in peat digging and sedge cutting. *Open:* Tuesdays–Saturdays 10.30 a.m.–5.00 p.m., Sundays 2.30 p.m.–4.30 p.m.

24 Norfolk Rural Museum

Beech House, Gressenhall, Dereham, Norfolk   *Gressenhall 563*
The life and work of the people of this premier agricultural county during the past 150 years is reflected in this extensive collection. Many of the agricultural tools and implements on display were manufactured locally. The museum incorporates a range of buildings, known as Craftsmen's Row, which contains a saddler's shop, a basket works, a smithy, a wheelwright's shop and a bakery. Other exhibits include steam engines and displays of local crafts and industries, and a small flock of New Norfolk Horn sheep can also be seen. The museum holds a number of special events throughout the summer.
Open: early May–late September, Tuesdays–Saturdays 10.00 a.m.–5.00 p.m., Sundays 2.00 p.m.–5.30 p.m.

25 Sotterley Agricultural Museum

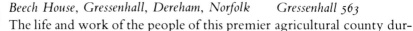

Alexander Wood Farm, Sotterley, Beccles, Suffolk   *Brampton 257*
Early tractors, stationary engines and an early threshing machine make up part of this varied collection of agricultural bygones. Many of the horsedrawn implements were made and used locally. The collection includes wooden ploughs, sail reapers and harrows, as well as wagons and carts. Among the selection of traps is a man trap.
Open: Easter–October, Sundays 1.00 p.m.–6.00 p.m.

26 Museum of East Anglian Life

Stowmarket, Suffolk   *Stowmarket 2229*
Among the reconstructed buildings in this partly open-air museum is the Alton Water Mill, which was saved from a watery grave when Tattingstone Valley was made into a reservoir; others include a fourteenth-century aisled hall discovered in a nearby village. The Grundisburgh smithy is in full working order and demonstrations are arranged from time to time, as are other old crafts and skills during the summer months.

A display of horsedrawn vehicles is housed in a Dutch barn, and a thirteenth-century barn holds a selection of agricultural implements.

Open: April–October, Mondays–Saturdays 11.00 a.m.–5.00 p.m.; Sundays 2.00 p.m.–5.00 p.m.

27   Easton Farm Park

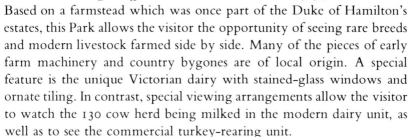

Easton, Woodbridge, Suffolk   Wickenham Market 746475

Based on a farmstead which was once part of the Duke of Hamilton's estates, this Park allows the visitor the opportunity of seeing rare breeds and modern livestock farmed side by side. Many of the pieces of early farm machinery and country bygones are of local origin. A special feature is the unique Victorian dairy with stained-glass windows and ornate tiling. In contrast, special viewing arrangements allow the visitor to watch the 130 cow herd being milked in the modern dairy unit, as well as to see the commercial turkey-rearing unit.

Open: April–September, 10.30 a.m.–6.00 p.m.

28   Museum of Country Bygones

High Street, Marton, Warwickshire   Leamington Spa 27030

All the agricultural items in this collection came from the immediate area of the village of Marton. The collection is made up of hand tools, and some examples of the work of country craftsmen including the wheelwright, the blacksmith and the shepherd. There is also a display of the general hand tools used by the farmworker in the field and barn – even the poacher is represented.

Open: Easter–October, daily 10.00 a.m.–8.00 p.m.

29   The Almonry Museum

Evesham, Worcestershire   Evesham 6944

A unique collection of implements, as the bulk of the items particularly relate to the local market gardening for which the Vale of Evesham is noted. The collection as a whole, which also includes hurdle-making and thatching tools, is aimed at reflecting local history.

Open: Good Friday–September, 2.30 p.m.–6.30 p.m., daily except Mondays and Wednesdays

30   Avoncroft Museum of Buildings

Stoke Prior, Bromsgrove, Worcestershire   Bromsgrove 31363

Many buildings of architectural and historic interest have been rescued and re-erected on this 15-acre site. These include local buildings such as a granary from Worcestershire, and buildings from other counties, such as the cock-fighting theatre from Shropshire. A windmill, restored to working order, is one of the few post mills remaining in the Midlands.

Demonstrations of rural trades and crafts take place on various occasions throughout the season.

Open: March–November 10.30 a.m.–5.30 p.m. (or dusk if earlier)

31   Bewdley Museum

Load Street, Bewdley, Worcestershire   Bewdley 403573
This is a specialist local history museum with an agricultural section which includes many photographs. The emphasis of the collection is on the crafts and industries associated with Bewdley and the Wyre Forest district, such as bark-peeling, tanning, saddlery, pewtering and horn-making. Demonstrations are sometimes given by the craftsmen who have studios in the museum.

Open: March–November, Mondays–Saturdays 10.00 a.m.–5.30 p.m.; Sundays 2.00 p.m.–5.30 p.m.

32   Acton Scott Working Farm Museum

Marshbrook, nr Church Stretton, Salop   Marshbrook 306/307
The aim of this unique county museum is to illustrate life and work on a nineteenth-century Shropshire upland farm. Occupying a range of eighteenth-century buildings and extending over 22 acres, the museum is stocked as a period mixed farm with breeds of horses, cows, sheep, pigs and poultry rarely seen today. The farm is worked using nineteenth-century arable techniques, the crops being grown on a traditional 4-course rotation. The visitor can watch butter being made, and there are craft demonstrations at weekends, while the Shire horses are worked every day, weather permitting.

Open: April, May, September, October, Mondays–Saturdays 1.00 p.m.–5.00 p.m., Sundays and Bank Holidays 10.00 a.m.–6.00 p.m.; June–August, Mondays–Saturdays 10.00 a.m.–5.00 p.m., Sundays and Bank Holidays 10.00 a.m.–6.00 p.m.

33   West Wales Farm Park

Blaenbedw Isaf, Plwmp, nr Llandyssul, Dyfed   Rhydlewis 317
There are over 75 species of rare animals and fowl housed within the 60 acres of this existing dairy farm. While particular emphasis is given to the preservation of the Belted Welsh and the White Welsh cattle, many other breeding groups of cattle, pigs, sheep, goats, poultry and horses can be seen. A 'Farming and Wildlife' walk affords good views of the coastline.

Open: May–September 10.00 a.m.–6.00 p.m.

34 Welsh Folk Museum

St Fagans, Cardiff   Cardiff 569441

This extensive and varied collection reflects the cultural and agricultural history of the Principality. The range of tools, implements and machines on display relate to the development of farming techniques within Wales, a theme which is extended by the collection of wagons and carts. The open-air section of reconstructed buildings, including a cornmill from Dyfed and a smithy from Powys, all help to illustrate the varied local character of the country.

Open: October–March 10.00 a.m.–5.00 p.m.; April–September 10.00 a.m. –6.00 p.m.

35 Cotswold Farm Park

Guiting Power, Cheltenham, Gloucestershire   Guiting Power 307

The Cotswold Farm Park is part of the arable farm run by Joe Henson and his partner John Neave, and here you can see a collection of rare historical breeds of farm animals which are no longer used in commercial agriculture. The stories behind these breeds are as fascinating as the animals themselves. Cart horses, and occasionally a team of oxen, can sometimes be seen working in and around the Park.

Open: 26 April–28 September 10.30 a.m.–6.00 p.m.

36 Manor Farm Museum

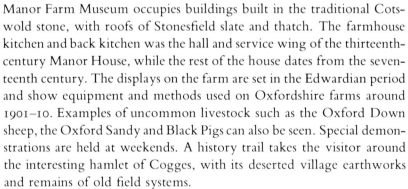

Cogges, Witney, Oxfordshire   Witney 72602

Manor Farm Museum occupies buildings built in the traditional Cotswold stone, with roofs of Stonesfield slate and thatch. The farmhouse kitchen and back kitchen was the hall and service wing of the thirteenth-century Manor House, while the rest of the house dates from the seventeenth century. The displays on the farm are set in the Edwardian period and show equipment and methods used on Oxfordshire farms around 1901–10. Examples of uncommon livestock such as the Oxford Down sheep, the Oxford Sandy and Black Pigs can also be seen. Special demonstrations are held at weekends. A history trail takes the visitor around the interesting hamlet of Cogges, with its deserted village earthworks and remains of old field systems.

Open: April–September 11.00 a.m.–6.00 p.m.

37 St Albans City Museum

Hatfield Road, St Albans, Hertfordshire   St Albans 56679

Agricultural implements, as such, represent only a small proportion of this collection. The rural life section however consists of what is reputed to be one of the best collections of craft tools in the country. Included in this are the tools of the saddler, the tanner, the farrier and the clog maker, as well as those of such local industries as straw-hat manufacture. The museum also embodies the reconstructed workshops of the blacksmith, the cooper and the wheelwright.

Open: Mondays–Saturdays 10.00 a.m.–5.00 p.m.

38   Old Mill House Museum

Mill Green, Hatfield, Hertfordshire   Hatfield 71362
A small museum which houses a wide-ranging collection illustrating various aspects of local life so dominated by the great Hatfield estates. Exhibits cover trades and crafts, homes and pastimes, as well as agriculture. Temporary exhibitions on other local themes can be seen from time to time. The watermill is also part of the museum. There are craft demonstrations during many of the weekends of the peak summer months.

Open: Tuesdays–Fridays 10.00 a.m.–5.00 p.m.; Saturdays, Sundays and Bank Holidays 2.00 p.m.–5.00 p.m.

39   Upminster Tithe Barn Agricultural and Folk Museum

Hall Lane, Upminster, Essex   Romford 44297
Displayed in a fifteenth-century timber and thatched barn, the strength of this collection is in its woodworking, plumbing, coopering and leather-working tools. The aim of the museum is to reflect the agricultural past of the area. Other exhibits include domestic bygones, farm tools and a fine nineteenth-century Essex wagon.

Open: weekends only, April–October 11.00 a.m.–1.00 p.m., 2.15 p.m.–5.30 p.m.

40   Wye College Agricultural Museum

Brook, Ashford, Kent   Wye 812401
Agricultural vehicles, implements and tools are housed in an early nineteenth-century barn and a nineteenth-century oasthouse, both buildings being of great historic importance. The oasthouse is of a unique design, and is partly sectioned inside so that the manner of its use can clearly be seen. Although the housed collection represents agriculture generally, it does have a strong local flavour. Of special interest are the wagons, the Kent ploughs, the seed drills and a very early tractor which was designed for work in the hop fields.

Open: May–September, Wednesdays only 2.00 p.m.–5.00 p.m.; August, Saturdays 2.00 p.m.–5.00 p.m.

41 Wilmington Priory

Wilmington, Polegate, Sussex   Alfriston 870537

Incorporated in the remains of a Benedictine priory, this small museum has a collection of agricultural implements traditional to the area and dating from the eighteenth to the early twentieth century. Close to the priory is the mysterious Long Man of Wilmington.

Open: April–September, Mondays, Wednesdays and Saturdays 10.00 a.m.–6.00 p.m.; Sundays 2.00 p.m.–5.00 p.m.

42 The Weald and Downland Open Air Museum

Singleton, nr Chichester, Sussex

This interesting collection of historic buildings has been saved from demolition and decay to be re-erected at Singleton. It includes a fifteenth-century farmhouse, a fourteenth-century house and an Elizabethan treadmill. Other interesting buildings to be seen are the nineteenth-century blacksmith's forge and a wheelwright's shop.

Open: 31 March–30 September, daily except non–Bank Holiday Mondays 11.00 a.m.–6.00 p.m.; October, Wednesdays and weekends 11.00 a.m.–5.00 p.m.; November–March, Sundays only 11.00 a.m.–4.00 p.m.

43 Queen Elizabeth Country Park

Gravel Hill, Horndean, nr Portsmouth, Hampshire   Horndean 595040

An extensive piece of worked countryside consisting of downland and woodland which embodies a wide range of exhibits and activities. The Forest and Woodland Craft Area contains static displays describing traditional woodland crafts and modern forestry. Demonstrations of wattle hurdle making and pit sawing can be seen during the summer months. The downland is grazed by sheep and cattle, including some of the rarer breeds, and demonstrations of shepherding can be seen at intervals. The Park encompasses an ancient farm set among many field antiquities.

Open (Park Centre): April–September 10.00 a.m.–6.00 p.m.; October, November and March closed Mondays, Saturdays and dusk; other periods Sundays only until dusk

44 Old Kiln Agricultural Museum

Reeds Road, Tilford, Farnham, Surrey   Frensham 2300

A collection of bygones reflecting agriculture based on the power of the horse. The exhibits include ploughs, furrows, binders and seed drills, with carts and wagons of several types. There are also displays covering horticulture and forestry, and a complete wheelwright's shop.

Open: April–September, Wednesdays to Sundays, and Bank Holidays 11.00 a.m.–6.00 p.m.

45   Museum of English Rural Life

University of Reading, Whiteknights, Reading, Berkshire   *Reading 85123*
(extn 475)
This expansive collection of mainly nineteenth- and early twentieth-century agricultural equipment is from all parts of the country and includes carts, wagons and household equipment. The collection of craft tools is said to be second to none. Other noted exhibits include the earliest surviving example of steam cultivating equipment.
Open: Tuesdays–Saturdays 10.00 a.m.–4.30 p.m.

46   Breamore Countryside Museum

Breamore, Hampshire   *Breamore 270/468*

The items in this museum are arranged to show the historical development of farming tools and machinery as they are related to the seasons of the year. The varied collection includes sections on transport and power, the rural industries and the smallholder. There is also a collection of livestock.
Open: April–September, daily except Mondays and Fridays (unless Bank Holidays) 2.00 p.m.–5.30 p.m.

47   Calbourne Water Mill and Rural Museum

Calbourne, Isle of Wight   *Calbourne 227*
When this mill ceased operation in 1955 it was decided to preserve it, as it stood, as an example of bygone agricultural days. Not only can the miller's implements be seen, along with the mill's machinery, but the museum has been extended to include other articles of past rural life.
Open: Easter–October 10.00 a.m.–6.00 p.m.

48   Somerset Rural Life Museum

Abbey Farm, Chilkwell Street, Glastonbury, Somerset   *Glastonbury 32903*
A museum which aims to illustrate the social, domestic and community life which went with the horsedrawn age of nineteenth-century agriculture. Every object in the collection was either made or used in Somerset. The strong regional character of the people is particularly well illustrated by the tools, equipment and history of the activities of Cheddar cheese making, withy growing and cider making. Of special interest is the 'John Hodges Story', the real-life story of this Victorian farm labourer, from birth to death.
Open: Easter–October, Mondays–Fridays 10.00 a.m.–5.00 p.m., Thursdays 10.00 a.m.–8.00 p.m., Saturdays and Sundays 2.00 p.m.–7.00 p.m.; November–Easter, Mondays–Fridays 10.00 a.m.–5.00 p.m., Saturdays and Sundays 2.30 p.m.–5.00 p.m.

49   James Countryside Museum

Bicton Gardens, East Budleigh, Devon   *Budleigh Salterton 3881*
Most of this collection is of West Country origin by use, make, or both. The collection of utensils, tools, implements and vehicles represents the transition from horse- to motor-powered farming, its aim being to reflect the effects of the industrial revolution on rural life.
Open: end of March–end of September 10.00 a.m.–6.00 p.m.

50   Tiverton Museum

Horsdon House, 23 Blundells Avenue, Tiverton, Devon   *Tiverton 2446*
The Agricultural Hall of this museum contains many items, some of which are specific to the area, including several rarities such as a seventeenth-century cider screw and a 'Norwegian' harrow believed to be the only one in existence. A village smithy, which operated for some 200 years, has been faithfully restored.
Open: daily except Bank Holidays and Christmas 10.30 a.m.–4.30 p.m.

51   Ashley Countryside Collection

Ashley House, Wembworthy, Chumleigh, Devon   *Ashreigney 226*
A collection of farmhouse and farm antiquities reflecting the progress and development of rural life, with particular reference to Devon; included are various types of horsedrawn plough. The major feature of the collection is the 40 different breeds of British sheep.
Open: Easter–September, Sundays, Mondays, Wednesdays and Saturdays 10.00 a.m.–6.00 p.m.; daily except Thursdays during August

52   Finch Foundry Museum

Sticklepath, Okehampton, Devon   *Sticklepath 286/352*
This museum is based on a unique nineteenth-century edge tool factory which operated, entirely powered by water, from 1814 up to 1960. Three working waterwheels drive a complex of tilt hammers, drop stamps, metal cutting shears and other machines once used to manufacture agricultural tools, many of which are on display.
Open: March–October 11.00 a.m.–5.30 p.m.

53   Helston Folk Museum

Old Butter Market, Church Street, Helston, Cornwall
Ranging over all aspects of the life of Helston and the surrounding district, the museum includes in its collection old farming implements and machinery, together with those of the associated cottage industries.
Open: daily except Bank Holidays and Flora Day (8 May) 10.30 a.m.–12.30 p.m., 2.00 p.m.–4.30 p.m. (closed 12.00 a.m. Wednesdays)

54   North Cornwall Museum and Gallery

The Clease, Cornwall   Camelford 3229

Rural life in North Cornwall from fifty to a hundred years ago is reflected in this collection. There are sections on farm machinery, as well as blacksmith's and wheelwright's tools. Other sections include cobbling, carpentry, pottery, and slate and granite quarrying. The museum contains a reconstruction of a turn of the century moorland cottage.
Open: April–September 10.30 a.m.–5.00 p.m., daily except Sundays

55   Wayside Museum

Zennor, St Ives, Cornwall   St Ives 6945

Tools and implements relating to traditional crafts and agriculture can be seen alongside those relating to other local crafts and industries, such as mining and fishing. The museum contains a good collection of ploughs, and the remains of an old watermill and forge can be seen, as can a typical Cornish kitchen with open hearth and baking oven.
Open: May–October 9.30 a.m.–dusk

The Wheelwright

BERNARD PRICE

A farm cart, said William Morris, was not designed to be decorative; but it was a beautiful object because it was made by craftsmen with a practical purpose in mind.

The craft of the wheelwright is as old as the wheel, and by the middle of the nineteenth century it had become among the most sophisticated of skills. The days of coaches and the great coaching roads would have been the heyday of the wheelwright, but nostalgia so often blinds us to the hardships of road travel in the past. For a passenger stranded by a broken wheel in open country between London and York the experience would have seemed like shipwreck.

The wheelwright relied upon the co-operation of the local blacksmith in order to complete his work, and even if their shops were not side by side they would always be close to one another. The marked modern revival of interest in farm carts, wagons, and the driving and showing of horse-drawn vehicles has injected new heart into the craft and created a new generation of wheelwrights.

For anyone wishing to understand the lore and skill of the wheelwright in any detail I recommend that classic book by George Sturt *The Wheelwright's Shop*. First published in 1923 and reprinted since, it is practical, sympathetic, and has the feel of true literature.

In the same way that the shoeing of a horse has been compulsive viewing for centuries, so too is the making of a wheel. The wheelwright's yard is full of carefully chosen timber, some of it left to season for years, but very carefully stacked in order that it should not warp. Like character actors certain timbers have particular roles in the making of a wheel. The spokes are of oak, cleft rather than sawn, and the cleaving is done in the summer by the woodman while the sap still runs through the length of the timber. The outer ring of the wheel is usually made up of six well-fitting sections, each section being called a felloe, although I have never yet heard a wheelwright who did not call them 'fellies'. Oak, ash, elm or beech can be used for the felloes. Cut from patterns, they were once the work of axe, adze and draw-knife, but the task has been made easier by the use of the band-saw and other power tools.

In the centre of the wheel is the nave, or hub, made of elm. A cylindrically shaped piece of elm, varying in size according to the wheel, is carefully marked out with compasses for drilling with an auger as a preliminary to being mortised for the spokes. This work requires strength as well as skill. The centre of the nave is bored out with a heavy hand tool called a boxing engine, and carries the iron box and axle.

When all the components of the wheel are ready for assembly, the spokes are hammered into the nave and tongued for the felloe, two spokes for each. Like many difficult things well done it all sounds astonishingly easy. The final stage is carried out on the tyring platform, a large circular slab of iron. The metal for the tyre is measured with a 'traveller', a disc of wood or iron that is first run round the rim of the wheel like a giant map measurer. The hot tyre is then shrunk on to the wheel and so binds the whole assembly tight.

Yet there is far more to it than that: an understanding of the materials and the handling of tools, from a cross-cut to a spokeshave, and a knowledge of wagon construction, balance and form. Like his wheels, the wheelwright is a man of many parts.

Gordon Beningfield, Bernard Price, Angela Rippon and Ted Moult admire the craftsmanship of the wheelwright who made this cartwheel now on display at Cogges Farm Museum.

The Shepherd

BERNARD PRICE

A shepherd's life was, and in many cases still is, a lonely one, but for many shepherds the solitary life is meat and drink. Once, when walking in Scotland and with darkness coming on, I found that the mountain path I was following had been washed away by rain. A diversion brought me to a small white-walled croft where I was welcomed by a young shepherd and his wife, who clearly revelled in their situation. Their tiny home was warm, they abounded in clear-eyed good health, and they were joyfully appreciative of the magnificent palisade of hills and mountains that enclosed their world. His crook, beautifully fashioned from a ram's horn, stood by the door, as splendid as a bishop's crozier.

The craft skills of the shepherd were, and are, many. Whole books have been written about them, but here I wish to draw attention to a handful of lesser-known aspects of the old shepherd's lore.

A fossil hunter from boyhood, I remember bringing home my first flint cast of a sea-urchin, which had left its imprint in stone for me to find, tens of millions of years later, on the chalk hills of Sussex. An uncle informed me that what I had found was called a 'shepherd's crown'. Why did it have such a name? He did not know, but I learned from an old shepherd at Yapton that he and his fellows had always collected them. They believed that such fossils were lucky and, in particular, would keep them safe from being struck by lightning and Neolithic burial sites have been discovered in which the remains were surrounded by 'shepherd's crowns'.

Many of the Downland shepherds, especially the younger ones, carried fifes. One of them, Harry Boniface, whom I did not meet until he was eighty-eight years old, told me that he could raise a tune and signal with it to other shepherd lads with distant flocks. 'We weren't supposed to do it,' he said, 'but it was grand to hear the sound of fifes drifting up across the woods from other hills.'

Mr Tom Rushbridge, shepherd of the Sussex Downs, photographed near Findon in the 1920s by Barclay Wills who used a box Brownie. In the background is Cisbury Ring.

Note the 'false tongues' – large pieces of thick leather fastened over the laces of his boots. These boots can now be seen in Worthing Museum.

The possessions of the old shepherds have left a thin detritus, evidence of a bygone age, scattered through curio shops, cottages and farms – sheep bells of many descriptions, lambing and dipping hooks, as well as the more familiar crooks, smocks and leggings, the broad umbrellas, and the horn lanterns which were no longer made after the First World War. Some time ago I was talking to an old farmworker at Coldwaltham and, before I left him, he hunted about in his garden shed and produced a heavy piece of wood shaped like a large catapult, and asked me if I knew what it was.

'That,' I said, 'is a sheep bow, and at one time you would have found one on every farm on and around the South Downs.'

'Yes,' said the old man, 'and do you know that they call them bilboes, but I don't know why.' In the Sussex dialect a natural forked branch of catapult shape is called a 'strod', but its heavier Y-shaped cousin is indeed called a 'bilbo' or 'bilboe'. When a show or fair was in the offing the pointed foot of the bilbo was rammed firmly into the earthen floor of the sheepshed. The shepherd then chose an animal from the flock and held it fast by securing its neck in the wooden 'V' by an iron rod across the top. With shears carefully sharpened he then clipped, trimmed and combed until the animal was fit to face the judges. Centuries ago, the name 'bilbo' was given by the Spaniards to fetters used on board their ships to restrain prisoners. These shackles were made of steel from Bilbao, hence the name. I wonder if it was some fortunate sailor turned shepherd who first brought such a shackle to his sheep?

The derivation of words delights philologists, and yet another poser thrown up by the shepherd is the ancient method of counting or 'telling' sheep. Once again there are regional differences to be found, just as there are in the shaping of crooks, but in Sussex sheep were counted in pairs as they passed through a hurdle, the shepherd notching a tally stick as he called aloud:

One-erum	*Shatherum*
Two-erum	*Wine-berry*
Cockerum	*Wagtail*
Shu-erum	*Tarrydiddle*
Shitherum	*Den*

The origins of such a counting system must indeed be remote.

I have found that most shepherds have a simple philosophy of life; the favourite comment of one, which I like very much, is: 'People are not so content nowadays, even with all they've got! Always rushing about, yet they have time to pick one another to pieces! They don't try to help one another, or put one another together a bit.'

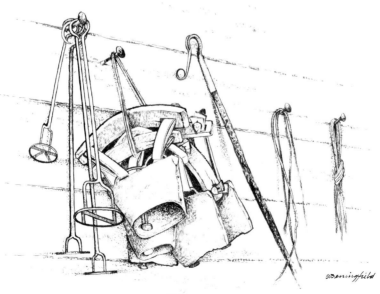

Thomas Bewick — A Countryman's Artist

GORDON BENINGFIELD

I remember being told, long before I ever dreamed of becoming a professional, that I wouldn't succeed as an artist unless I first became a craftsman. Until I was a skilled draughtsman I would never be able to make pictures; until I could draw well, I would never be able to paint. It was good advice. Not only did it make a world of difference to my own efforts, but it helped me appreciate the work of other artists. When I look at the work of Thomas Bewick I am reminded that not only was he a superb artist but, above all, he was a great craftsman. He was also a man with acute powers of observation. Although he was very much a part of the countryside in which he lived and worked, he was able to stand back from it and record it faithfully and honestly. It is, I think, these qualities that make him my hero.

As a boy on his father's farm at Cherryburn outside Newcastle upon Tyne, Thomas lived the kind of country life that I would have enjoyed. It was the middle of the eighteenth century and the countryside looked just like the scenes we now put on Christmas cards. The village schoolmaster tried to beat Latin and Greek into the young Bewick, but Thomas preferred to play truant, spending much of his time down by the river Tyne fishing for trout and perch, or up in the woods trapping birds, or in winter hunting hares across the snow-covered fields. At the end of the day he would make his way back to Cherry-burn, hoping that his father would not be waiting to give him one of his regular hidings for wasting time. But Thomas never wasted a minute; he had been attending his own private school, the countryside itself. It's here that he learned to observe and then record – drawing on anything he could find, even the tombstones in Ovingham churchyard. He had no formal training in art, and certainly no special instruction in natural history. He was self-taught, and it was no doubt on these illicit rambles that he developed these unique powers of observation that shaped his life and his work.

After leaving school Bewick completed seven years' apprenticeship to a jobbing engraver in Newcastle. Here he learned his craft. Woodcutting, which had reached its peak in the fifteenth century, particularly in Germany, was now seldom used for anything more sophisticated than playing cards and pamphlets; good quality books were illustrated with elegant copperplate engravings which were printed quite separately from the text. Bewick's fascination and affinity with wood might have been his downfall, had it not been for a new demand for children's books. Newcastle was enjoying a sudden prosperity, which included book publishing on a scale second only to London. Ralph Beilby, to whom Bewick was apprenticed, was at one time the only engraver in Newcastle, and he cornered the market – including commissions for woodcut illustrations for children's books. The clumsy woodcuts were thought quite adequate for children, and Bewick did them all, soon outclassing his employer. He drew on the images of his own childhood, still vivid to him, to delight the eyes and minds of children in distant towns.

Bewick's illustrations for Gay's *Fables* won him an award while he was still an apprentice, and it may have been this that brought him to the attention of Isaac Taylor, one of the most celebrated and influential illustrators of the time. Taylor adopted the budding Bewick as his protégé and set him up in London, where he worked almost exclusively in the more fashionable medium of copper. Whether it was this or his obvious dislike of high society in London that decided him, Bewick soon packed his bags and went back to Newcastle, convinced that he would rather be poor than live a lie to his work and his country upbringing. But although I'm sure he didn't know it then, or perhaps ever, Bewick, by his stubborn loyalty to the woodcut, identified himself with the new Romantic movement, which was to become much more influential

than any of the contemporary trends in the south of England. After Bewick, and in similar vein, came the Norwich school of rural landscape painting epitomised by John Sell Cotman and John Crome, and a few years later of course came John Constable. These are artists I admire enormously, and all, I believe, were influenced by Bewick's achievements in wood.

To call his craft woodcutting is not to do it justice. Although Bewick himself described it as such, the technique he revived and perfected was really wood engraving. He worked with a graver on the hard, tight end-grain of the wood, rather than cutting into the plank side with a knife, and thus created a crispness in wood that was otherwise only achieved in metal. The combination of this technique and the natural grain of wood gave his work a textured quality that complemented the country subjects he chose to portray. Somehow in lifeless metal they would not have been so real.

Back in Newcastle, Bewick became a partner in the firm in which he had served his apprenticeship. Now he was his own master and could largely choose his subjects but, given such freedom, it is surprising how slowly his major works appeared. His *A General History of Quadrupeds* came out in 1790 (with text by Beilby) and the two volumes of *A History of British Birds* followed in 1797 and 1804. For me the bird books are his masterpieces. The giraffes and elephants which he drew for *Quadrupeds* were obviously alien to him, and the stuffed specimens he copied in Wycliffe Museum must have been less than perfect for a man who had spent all his life watching wild animals in the open air. Birds, however, were old friends, part of the country scene in which he grew up, and this shows in his studies for *British Birds*. So often he portrayed them against the familiar backdrop of Cherryburn farm or some other landmark that would have been obvious only to those who knew and loved his private world. For the rest of us, these cameos have come to represent everything that was good about eighteenth-century rural England.

The species which he could not see in the wild for himself were sent to him by friends from all over the British Isles, and he set about engraving them with a diligence and sensitivity which had never been seen before in natural history illustration. I know how difficult it is to portray plumage and how lifeless it can look. Bewick mastered such subtleties as only a countryman could, and all of it cut in wood. It's difficult to believe, when looking at his books today, that every illustration was printed from his original blocks.

But Bewick was not content to show wildlife in its simple natural setting; he started to dramatise the backdrop. Little incidents began to creep into his illustrations – mere hints at first, and then full-blown country dramas. The poacher and his dog; the boys playing leapfrog over the gravestones in the churchyard; the cowman avoiding the toll bridge by wading through the river holding the poor cow's tail; the cat stuck up the tree; the drunken farmer

staggering back home from the inn. Bewick was so pleased with these impressions of the day-to-day reality of country life that he included them as illustrations in their own right, often at the end of each description of a species or group of birds. He called these delightful vignettes his 'tailpieces', and each one tells a story, often of human hardship. They are not sentimental or romantic – simply accurate observations of country people at work and play. The discipline he needed to watch wildlife could not have been very different from that needed to observe people. Although he was very much a part of the country community, he was also a detached observer who could depict accurately what he saw. That is the job of an artist, to be objective and yet sympathetic. Bewick showed the blunt, often bawdy, side of country life, but he was never critical or unkind. I'm sure that his friends would have recognised themselves in his tailpieces, and would have enjoyed the little incidents he showed. One of my favourites is the scene outside the inn, where almost all the men of the village seem to be gathered in a circle, encouraging the competitors in some illicit sport such as a cockfight, perhaps, or enjoying a scrap between two suitors. We shall never know, but I'm sure that the men of Cherryburn remembered the event well.

His choice of subjects for these tailpieces reveals as much about Bewick himself as it does about his countryside. I feel I know him well, and that his talents would be equally welcome today. I wonder what, two hundred years later, he would choose to portray in our countryside. Certainly he would be struck by the change, the disappearance of the small fields and woods, the tampering with our streams and rivers and the severity of our farmland. He would probably be horrified by the amount of traffic through the country lanes and by the impact of machinery on the shape of the countryside itself. But he would find that much of rural England is the same – just that there is not so much of it. There are still many villages in Britain where life is carried on much as it was around Cherryburn. Boys still play leapfrog over gravestones and farmers still come home from the pub – at least they do in my village. Although we've got combines and reversible ploughs, silos and electric fences, there is nothing basically different about the way we live. It's undoubtedly an easier life, and there's more time to enjoy the countryside itself, but I often feel that the modern countryman overlooks the greatest asset on his doorstep, perhaps because he has grown up with it. Many times I have found myself enthusing about some corner of our village or some natural marvel that no one else has noticed. When their attention is drawn to it, they begin to see for themselves. Perhaps that is the role of the artist in the countryside – to be a kind of outsider, who can stand back from his familiar environment and look at it afresh. For me, it's dandelion clocks and brambles, old gate-posts and beds of stinging nettles, cobwebs and butterflies.

Bewick's story-telling tailpieces have now become classics of eighteenth-century English country life; they are almost clichés. But unlike many of the romantic artists who followed, he was neither sentimental nor idealistic. His engravings were true to life, and were as convincing and appealing to country people as they were to his patrons in towns.

Bewick never retired from work, even if he could have afforded to. He found the countryside an endless source of inspiration, and discovered a way of conveying his enthusiasm to others. By portraying it so honestly at a time when many of his contemporaries were flocking to the towns, he drew attention to the details of the life they were leaving behind, and did more, perhaps, than any other artist to ensure that it survived.

Whose Countryside Is It Anyway?

PHIL DRABBLE

Every competent naturalist knows that the human species is as territorially aggressive as any badger. Intruders to the caves of our prehistoric ancestors were doubtless clobbered over the head with a heavy club. Tribal wars would have been fought for the best pasture or hunting ground and violent hands laid on those who dared dispute the victors' spoils. At the other end of the scale, weaklings would have muttered that the countryside was theirs and joined forces with their fellows in their efforts to stake a claim on the land of their dreams.

There are still two camps, the Haves and the Have Nots. If you are lucky enough to live in a cottage in the country, you probably spit fire at every stranger who raises the echoes with his noisy motor bike, or strolls by your garden gate with his transistor radio polluting the air with pop music. But if your rural retreat is still wreathed in the smoke of your pipe dreams, the chances are that you only see the countryside in your precious hours of leisure. This will give you a different point of view and you may well find yourself waving your banner at the head of protestors, hell-bent on stopping a line of pylons stitching their way across green fields to bestow the boon of comforting instant heat and light on those who work as well as play among the rigours of rural life, whatever the weather.

Sportsmen on grouse moors resent their birds being flushed by the local rambling club as bitterly as the ramblers condemn farmers who are earning their living by ploughing furrows across public paths. The interests of fishermen and power boaters, rally drivers and horsemen are inevitably opposed.

Human nature has not changed. A thousand years ago King Canute granted the right of every Freeman to take game or vert (green wood) on his own territory, but without the right of Chase, and 'let all abstain from mine, wherever I may wish to have it'. To give bite to his commands, Canute imposed a fine of twice the value of the game for the first two convictions, while a third-time offender forfeited all he was worth to the King. If an offender 'by coursing or hunting, shall force a Royal beast, which the English call staggon, to pant or be out of breath, a Freeman shall lose his liberty for a year, if an unfreeman, for two years and a bondsman shall be declared an outlaw'. Canute's forest laws continued: 'if any of them shall kill such a Royal beast, the Freeman shall lose his freedom, the other his liberty and the bondsman his life.'

So the Normans, who are widely supposed to have introduced the harsh forest laws, were not the pioneers; they simply continued and perhaps elaborated what the Danes had begun. Even the clergy were a sporting bunch in those days – the Bishop of Lichfield was always getting into hot water for poaching on royal preserves in the area where I now live.

Most of England in medieval times was uncultivated and ideal for hunting. Huge tracts of land were designated 'forest' – only the King had the power to do this – and were 'maintained for the wild beasts of the forest, chase and warren'. The boundaries, or meeres, were fixed and widely known, and the stringent forest laws were enforced by forest officers.

The purpose of the laws was to protect the 'beasts of the forest' and the vert. The vert included every tree or bush of the forest which supplied food or shelter for the deer, and was subdivided into 'special vert', including fruit-bearing trees such as beech, oak, crab, pear, etc., 'over vert' and 'nether vert'. The beasts of the forest were the hart and hind (red deer), the buck and doe (fallow deer), the hare, the boar and the wolf. Although England was sparsely populated, the laws concerning what was and was not permissible in the countryside were rigidly enforced – and ignorance was no excuse.

Most country communities enjoyed some rights on common land and could collect turf and fuel and graze beasts, including pigs, which were allowed into the wood at acorn-time. This was the right of pannage and was vitally important not only to the owner of the pigs, but to those who owned cattle or horses too. Most creatures – from mice and squirrels, pheasants and pigeons, to cattle and horses – love acorns, but in excess they can be poisonous. Pigs, however, can tolerate them very well and fatten beautifully when there are plenty of acorns in their diet. So herds of pigs, scrumping through the woods in autumn, soon mopped up any dangerous surplus, and trod a few uneaten ones into the ground to survive as oak trees for the future.

Although local communities were allowed to go into the forest to collect fuel and tend their cattle, even they had to keep out in the 'Fence Month', the month of June. This is the season when the deer have their young, and it was considered far more important that woods were kept undisturbed at this time than that a few yokels should be able to romp about at will.

A chase was next in importance to a forest and was also usually designated by the King, who did not hesitate to lay waste whole farms and villages if that would improve the sporting amenities. The major difference between a chase and a forest was that noblemen were allowed to hunt in a chase. Every year there were ceremonial 'perambulations', when whole communities marched the boundaries of both forests and chases so that nobody had the slightest excuse for poaching in ignorance.

The noblemen themselves also owned parks, which were totally enclosed by deer-proof fences. Deer were kept in these parks not as ornamental amenities, as they are today, but so that they could be killed and eaten in winter when other fresh meat was scarce. The owners of such deer parks did not have to rely on breeding a surplus to kill. The King could grant them the right to build a deer leap on the boundary between their park fence and the forest; a hollow would be dug on the park side so that, from the park, the fence was high enough to be unjumpable, and a ramp put up to it on the forest side so that deer coming up to the edge of the park could jump down but could not jump back. One landowner on Cannock Chase, near where I live, still has the right to erect a deer leap which was granted to his ancestors by Edward II.

So in feudal times the King went – and hunted – where he chose and noblemen went and hunted where they chose, provided they avoided the Royal Forests. The rest of the populace could go more or less where they liked provided that they didn't interfere with the sport of their betters – and provided, also, they didn't even disturb the deer in their critical breeding season. Such rights were in fact little more than academic, because the common folk had to work such long hours that they can have had little leisure time.

The real change came when woodlands were cleared for agriculture during the time of the enclosures. Tracts of woodland gave way to isolated farms, and many of the workers lived in nearby village communities and walked to work across the fields, making footpaths along the most convenient line of country.

Before hard turnpike roads, metalled with broken stone, were laid, there had been a relatively small number of ancient trackways along which cattle had been driven and essentials such as salt carried on pack horses' backs. These ancient ways had been used freely by the community as 'rights of way' and many of them are immediately obvious because they go on for miles in relatively straight lines, since there was no question of the consent of individual owners when they were first trodden. G.K. Chesterton's claim that 'the rolling English drunkard made the rolling English road' is poetic licence; for the most part rolling English roads follow farm or parish or other boundaries, which are rarely straight, or have been dictated by specific physical features.

Footpaths were originally worn by working feet in days when leisure activities were the luxury of the few, and when day was done, the majority preferred to rest rather than cavort about the countryside for pleasure. When the country was populated by close-knit communities most of whose members were relations, neighbours or workmates, it was natural to give them permission to take short cuts across one's land. These paths, leading to the village school, pub or church, or nearest market town, gradually became accepted by all as traditional rights of way and the law now is that such a path, if used for twenty years without objection by the landowner, becomes a legal right of way which nobody can challenge.

Nowadays every large-scale map is criss-crossed by a network of footpaths and bridle paths which anyone can use as of right. Footpaths, as their name implies, are for people on foot and nothing else. Bridle paths can be used by people on foot or horseback, but may not be used by wheeled vehicles. (Except, believe it or not, perambulators, which are specifically allowed on footpaths although even cycles are excluded.) Bridle paths must be eight feet wide and have gates at least five feet wide, so you'd be all right on a carthorse; but there is no legally required width for a footpath.

As far as the law is concerned a public path, or highway, can only have been created in two ways. The simplest was by statute; when an award for the enclosure of common land was originally made, it sometimes included provision for a public highway across the enclosed land – this might be a footpath, bridle way or highway for wheeled vehicles. The second way was for the highway to be specifically created by other Act of Parliament.

Apart from highways established by statute, the law maintains that all others must have been created by dedication or acceptance. Acceptance is indicated by unchallenged use for a continuous period of at least twenty years. To avoid this, some landowners close the paths over their land for one day a year and advertise the fact locally and by a notice on the spot. This is a sensible precaution where a landowner does not mind his land being crossed but wishes to reserve the right to prevent it if the privilege is misused.

The fact that a path is marked on a map does not necessarily mean that it is a *public* path. Public footpaths should be marked on the Ordnance Survey maps as coloured dotted lines (red on the 1:50,000 Land Ranger series, and green on the 1:25,000 Pathfinder series). Access roads to houses and farms and woodland rides are also marked but carry no right of public access.

Where a legal footpath does cross private land, it gives the public the inalienable right to cross it, but not to digress from it, or to allow dogs to wander and disturb game or stock, or to pick wild flowers that are protected by law. The law, however, is traditionally an ass. It is not an offence to pick 'wild' mushrooms in a field, but the law does not explain how one reaches any that do not grow within reach of the public path. If the owner can prove that he planted some cultivated mushrooms as a crop, it would be stealing to pick the mushrooms in that field.

But we are no longer a rural community, and the increased population lives mostly in towns. Crowds and pressure of work and unpleasant urban surroundings induce the urge to escape to quieter places where the pace does not seem so hot. Easy transport and increasing leisure time have combined to send an avalanche of visitors to the countryside eager to 'get away from it all' and enjoy the charms of our wide open spaces. As a result, farmers and landowners no longer know personally the people who use the footpaths that cross their land. The pleasure of exchanging the time of day and local gossip with neighbours has been replaced by the sight of strangers wandering around the land without permission – because no permission is needed and they are there by legal right.

However amicable relationships may have been when most countrymen knew their neighbours personally, there are now few customs more fraught with potential friction than public rights of way. The unreasonable action of trampling growing crops to prove a point is often matched by equally unreasonable behaviour on the part of the folk who own the land.

A common deterrent was to put a bull in fields through which legal footpaths ran, accompanied by the notice BEWARE OF THE BULL. It concentrated visitors' minds wonderfully, often achieving the object of persuading them to go and play in someone else's yard. So in many counties it was made illegal to have a loose bull in a field through which a public path ran.

One crafty farmer hit the headlines with a device to get round this; he put a large ring through the nose of a shaggy Highland heifer. Her coat was so long that it was difficult even for the knowledgeable to see what it concealed and whether the creature was a cow or a bull. Few townsfolk hung around for long enough to find out. The ring through the nose was clue enough for them. Another reluctant host still keeps his beehives near the stile leading to his property and shakes them well on Sunday before he goes to church. His furious bees hang around all day waiting for their revenge, which they wreak on any hapless traveller who dares to cock his leg over 'their' stile. They are a far more effective deterrent than the most furious bull.

It all boils down to the basic territorial aggressions of our ancestors. Those who own or farm the land tend to be jealous of any intrusion, as ready to see off interlopers as any fighting cock on his muckheap, or guard dog in his yard. On the other side of the fence, it is natural for those who are unlucky enough to be forced to live in towns to feel that Britain is a free country and that it is their heritage to breathe fresh air and enjoy the scenery and wild flowers and bird song.

Perhaps both sides are too ready to climb on their high horses? Perhaps, with sensible compromise, there is room for both points of view, since not all farmers are threatening ogres, hell-bent on denying others what they regard most dear themselves, and not all townsfolk are pantomime explorers with rucksacks big enough to mount an expedition to Mars. If each recognised the black sheep who brings his own side into disrepute, there would be plenty of room for compromise.

Whatever the law says about 'rights', I regard it as a privilege to wander over another man's land and I behave as I would wish a visitor to my house to behave. If I owned a field of standing corn, I should be as furious as any man if someone deliberately trod it down. Growing crops for food comes higher on my list of priorities than taking a stroll for pleasure.

But it is surely not unreasonable to allow visitors to walk round the edge of the crop till it is cut and to make good the original path as soon as possible after ploughing? Rights of way across the country need not be inflexible to the point where it is only they that are in step. As farming fashions change, almost always in the direction of ever larger fields, it could often be of natural advantage to rationalise the traditional footpath network, diverting paths along headlands and other features that could well be more interesting than tramping across endless prairies of plough.

I read an account recently by the leader of a footpath preservation society, who was delighted to have obtained a grant out of rates to help open up a network of paths that had fallen into disuse for the simple reason that nobody had wanted to use them. He finished his story with the sad little aside that vandals had discovered the new ways into country they didn't know before and that they had done considerable damage. He seemed to consider the damage to someone else's land of small account against the gain in his own stamping ground. It so happens that some of the wildest and most beautiful scenery and some of the most exciting wildlife and satisfying solitudes are found on the least productive farming land. Wild and rugged mountains and superb moorland and heath are difficult terrain from which to wrest a living.

Every year an increasing acreage is being claimed for forestry and there is little doubt that, in an oil-less future, home-grown food and timber will be valued ever more highly. Hunting and shooting and fishing are all growth industries in the countryside, and all but huntsmen expect to pay for the privilege. For some reason that I have never understood, huntsmen and walkers expect to have the right to enjoy themselves wherever they choose for nothing. In a highly competitive society this has always seemed strange to me. If shooting men are prepared to rent land for their sport from a farmer, it is difficult to see why fox hunters think that they should be entitled to gallop through the coverts and disturb other people's game for nothing. The Forestry

National Trust property at Glencoyne. The new farm buildings have been constructed using traditional materials to merge with the natural surroundings.

Commission obtains some of its revenue by letting fishing, deer-stalking and camping facilities. It even makes forest tracks available for competitive motor trials and rallies, from which it also subsidises its costs.

Many farms on marginal land are now becoming uneconomic. It is vital to explore every possibility of augmenting our precarious livelihood and since these farms are so often set in superb country it might well be possible for tourism, including facilities for walking, climbing and bird-watching, to be one of the crops they could reap.

Some modern planning authorities pedal the doctrine of 'multi-use' of land, claiming that people should be able to pursue a wide range of interests on land and water. It rarely works. Speed-boating and bird-watching are obviously incompatible. There is a predictable outcry when motorcyclists wish to trail-ride over the solitudes of ancient trackways , while large numbers of orienteers surging through a forest containing herds of deer will obviously drive them out on to farmland where they will damage crops, or on to roads where motorists will damage them.

It is surely better, though less attractive to planners because it may not catch so many votes, that land should be zoned. Racing motorboats can go just as fast on reclaimed gravel pits as they can on some beautiful and secluded lake. Orienteers can as easily avoid getting lost in a forest where deer and wild birds do not abound as they can in an ornithologists' mecca. And walkers are likely to get more spiritual satisfaction in wild and arid country than they can by tramping over farmland.

There will always be those who retain the primitive territorial instincts of their forebears and raise their hackles if a stranger crosses their path, and those who seek to assert their 'rights' when a gentle reminder of privilege would have turned away wrath much more surely. Fortunately, however, they are in the minority. Most people are prepared to give as well as take. In a world of increasing pressures as well as increasing leisure there is room to play as well as to work in the countryside, and the simple pleasures it has to offer are coming to be valued ever more widely.

Britain's Most Lovely Walk

PETER CRAWFORD

Back in the 1920s, at a place and on a date unknown to us, a handful of celebrated country writers met at a symposium and waxed lyrical about our countryside. Masefield was there, and so was Hilaire Belloc. How they spent their time and what they said to each other that had not already been penned at length, I cannot guess; but one scrap of evidence came to light recently when Bernard Price, foraging in a manuscript dealer's shop in the West End of London, unearthed this original.

Symposium: "Britain's Most Lovely Walk"

Hilaire Belloc Esq.

It is very difficult to choose, but I think on the whole the most remarkable eight miles I know, which can only be seen walking or riding were those on the Stane Street, from near St Eartham in Sussex to Hardham. Since the Nore wood was cut down in the war only the last part of it, from Gumber corner onwards preserves the old character. If this destruction has too much spoilt these eight miles, then my next choice would be the walk from Burpham, close by, over the Downs to Storrington by way of Parham house.

Signature: ..H Belloc............

Clearly the assembled writers had been asked to give their candid opinion on which was Britain's loveliest walk. I doubt whether many of us could single out a favourite and, according to the West End dealer, nor could most of the distinguished company. Only Hilaire Belloc made a bold choice, and even he offered an alternative.

I know both walks well. As a boy I explored Sussex on my bike; from my home in West Chiltington I got to know the river Arun, Stane Street and the Downs above Storrington, and the Amberley wild brooks better than any part of Britain I've been to since. If Britain's most lovely bike ride counts, then I agree with Belloc!

There are approximately 100,000 miles of public paths in England and Wales, let alone the great tracks across the Border in Scotland. It has been estimated that they occupy no more than 30,000 acres of what might otherwise be productive farmland. Whatever the arguments, it seems a small price to pay for such an invaluable amenity which can be enjoyed by everyone. But, as Phil Drabble points out in his discussion of our rights in the countryside, many of these paths were created by local people for local use; it would be inconsiderate of us to insist on mass access. Better by far to concentrate on the more formal routes traversing the length and breadth of Britain, which link most of the special beauty spots and places of interest and skirt round areas that are intensively worked. This was the thinking behind the creation by the Countryside Commission in 1949 of the first Long Distance Path. There are now eight of these (nine if you count the recently approved Wolds Way, and ten including the long-awaited West Highland Way in Scotland). The map on page 180 shows where they run; they tend to be concentrated in upland or coastal areas, and in particular within National Parks.

It must give a tremendous sense of achievement to walk the complete length of one path, and I've heard of people who have stoically walked all of them. But the Long Distance Paths should also be able to accommodate the more casual country lover, who is content with a few miles of rambling rather than a marathon hike. Sadly some of the routes take one so far from public transport that it is often necessary to retrace one's steps before nightfall. There are, of course, several ways of overcoming this (an obliging friend waiting at the other end with a car, two cars strategically left at opposite ends of the chosen route, splitting the walking party into two and walking in opposite directions, and so on) but somehow they all seem to defeat the object of the exercise – unless exercise is the only object.

More attractive in many ways are the fifty or so paths now designated Short Distance Paths, which were created unofficially by enthusiasts, using existing rights of way. Some have been waymarked and all of them have guidebooks.

Phil Drabble and his German pointer Tick exploring the Cleveland Way in Yorkshire. Here the Long Distance Path crosses the river Rye alongside a very 'cottagey' cottage. 'We who don't have the luck to live in such desirable spots can still enjoy and be grateful for them when we find them.'

In spite of the visitors who flock to the Lake District the hills that have inspired generations of romantic poets remain essentially a working landscape. Billy Bowes and his family have farmed Herdwick sheep above Eskdale for nearly two centuries.

Modern demands on the British countryside have necessitated a different use for many of its traditional buildings. Flatford Mill, made famous by the paintings of John Constable, is now a Field Studies Centre.

Today's countryside is as beautiful as ever; there is simply not enough of it to satisfy all our rural aspirations.

It is best to browse in a bookshop to find just what would suit your needs, but some of the best known publishers of footpath guides are:

Cicerone Press, Harmony Hall, Milnthorpe, Cumbria LA7 7QA
Constable and Co Ltd, 10 Orange St, London WC2H 7EG
Cordee, 249 Knighton Church Rd, Leicester LE2 3JQ
Dalesman Publications, Clapham, Lancashire
Footpath Publications, Adstock Cottage, Adstock, Buckingham MK18 2HZ
The Ramblers' Association, 1–4 Crawford Mews, York St, London W1H 1PT
Shire Publications Ltd, Cromwell House, Church St, Princes Risborough, Aylesbury, Buckinghamshire HP17 9AJ
Spurbooks Ltd, 6 Parade Court, Bourne End, Buckinghamshire
Stile Publications, Mercury House, Otley, West Yorkshire LS21 3HE
Thornhill Press, 46 Westgate St, Gloucester
Westmorland Gazette, Stricklandgate, Kendal, Cumbria

The Countryside Commission (John Dower House, Crescent Place, Cheltenham, Gloucestershire) publishes useful leaflets on each of the Long Distance Paths, and has produced more comprehensive publications about some of them.

A lot of people are finding a happy compromise. They select a Long Distance Path, read up about it, and then devise their own itinerary to take in the features that particularly appeal to them, plus a detour or two along roads or other public ways that might take them off the straight and narrow. As Phil Drabble will tell you, it's not cheating to get on a bus or train! Footpaths are for enjoyment, not for testing one's endurance or breaking records. We should use them to suit our own tastes.

Several of our contributors to *In the Country* were persuaded to walk one of the paths (or a part of it) and their trips appeared as small films in the television series. Here Phil Drabble, Bernard Price and Tom Weir recall their impressions of the walks they took and give their different opinions on the whole question of Long Distance Paths. Each of us has our own preference, and I'm sure that every path in Britain is someone's loveliest walk.

Long Distance Paths

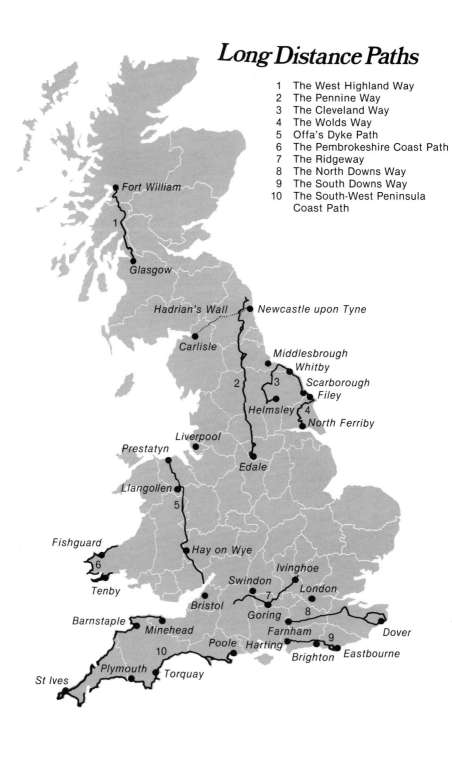

1 The West Highland Way
2 The Pennine Way
3 The Cleveland Way
4 The Wolds Way
5 Offa's Dyke Path
6 The Pembrokeshire Coast Path
7 The Ridgeway
8 The North Downs Way
9 The South Downs Way
10 The South-West Peninsula
    Coast Path

Fort William

Glasgow

Hadrian's Wall   Newcastle upon Tyne

Carlisle

Middlesbrough
Whitby
Scarborough
Filey
Helmsley
North Ferriby

Liverpool

Prestatyn

Llangollen

Edale

Fishguard

Hay on Wye

Ivinghoe

Swindon   London

Tenby

Bristol

Barnstaple   Goring

Minehead   Farnham   Dover

Poole   Harting

Plymouth   Torquay   Brighton   Eastbourne

St Ives

The Cleveland Way

PHIL DRABBLE

When I walk in the country, I reckon two's a crowd. However closely in tune I and my companion may be, he always seems to fidget and drive off some shy bird while I am watching it, and even the nicest female never knows when to stop talking!

Luckily such strictures only apply to the human race. Although I may seem an anti-social loner, the fact is that I never go far without my dog. Tick is a German short-haired pointer, affectionate and biddable, who is the perfect companion for a country walk. She never speaks out of turn, never chases anything unless I tell her to, and her hearing, scent and sight are so acute that they put my dull senses in the lowest clodhopper class by comparison. She stops at bushes and thickets to point out nesting birds or hidden animals that I should otherwise have passed by in ignorance.

When Peter Crawford invited me to explore an unfamiliar piece of country along the Cleveland Way, in North Yorkshire, and share the experience with television viewers, I naturally took Tick. The Cleveland Way was Britain's second Long Distance Path. It is in the North Yorkshire National Park and was opened in 1969.

Tick and I went by bus to Helmsley, which is a pleasant small market town, but neither of us likes the constraint of being attached to our respective ends of a dog lead and so we were both glad to escape out of the town to a footpath, where traffic was no longer a hazard and Tick could run free.

Rievaulx Abbey, a few hundred yards off the track, is a timeless ruin that restores my faith in continuity. It was erected by monks to the glory of God and, in spite of the fact that vandals of an earlier age knocked much of it down, the remaining ruins will still proclaim their builders' faith long after we are dust. But, however inspiring such mellow monuments to past faith may be, their attractions pall for me when I have to queue to see the details of their craftsmanship. So Tick and I moved on.

Half a mile further, where the track crosses the river Rye, a cottage with a superb, 'cottagey' garden nestles on the river bank as if the house owed nothing to human artistry but had grown as naturally as the trees that shelter it. It is such an eye-catcher that one instinctively stops on the bridge to gape into someone else's privacy. We who don't have the luck to live in such desirable spots can still enjoy and be grateful for them when we find them.

Roseberry Topping, a worthwhile detour from the main route of the Cleveland Way. At the foot of the hill is Great Ayton with refreshment for the less energetic.

This pause prompted Tick and me to forsake the popular way, wander along a forest track and sit on the bank of a stream sharing a block of chocolate, which is half the pleasure of spending a day in such congenial company.

In the afternoon we savoured the distant view of the White Horse above Kilburn from the top of Sutton Bank, and left the admiring crowds behind as we walked the Drover's Way, where other men and their dogs had driven cattle in generations past. Neither Tick nor I are gluttons for punishment and we saw no point in wearing our feet to blisters simply to boast that we'd walked the whole of the Way. We picked and chose what we wanted to see in the least populous spots, going by bus to Great Ayton and skirting Roseberry Topping on foot – but not climbing it. At the Rip-van-Winkle station of Kildale we jumped on the train, to fill our eyes with pleasure at the superb views along the Esk valley, and finally arrived at the ancient port of Whitby after a day neither of us would mind repeating time and time again – in the same company.

Walking the Sussex Downs

BERNARD PRICE

I like to walk for a period of days rather than hours, but even the briefest stroll gives me an opportunity to relax and to enjoy the fresh air and scenery, the favourite plants of each season and the wildlife as well as giving much-needed exercise. When I am at home and working at my desk it becomes the highlight of the day simply to pick up a stick and walk down to the village pond and back. I usually walk in late afternoon, for at that time of day the pond in my village, flanked by the church, the manor farm and open fields, is reminiscent of a busy waterhole. Mallard flight in and out; the rector locks up the church for the night; and the tractors croak their way back to the cart-sheds like copper-throated cock pheasants going up to roost.

If I did not linger I would be home again in twenty-five minutes, but there is always something more to see or a local countryman to talk to. Last winter for the first time I saw a hen-harrier hunting low over these fields, and two days after that first sighting I discovered that a pair of them had made their winter refuge in New Barn, a great flint-built grain cupboard that was already old when Queen Victoria was crowned. It is impossible to grow tired of such a favourite walk, for it is its very familiarity that enables me to note the changes and surprises it continually offers.

There are many people who say to me 'Why don't we see the interesting things that you do when you go for a walk?' I can only tell them that what I and so many others enjoy is there for all to see; it simply requires the right, patient approach. So few people now use their senses to the full, or are able to understand and appreciate what they do see. I have many times met families returning to their cars after denuding whole hillsides of cowslips and the small areas of orchids that grow among them. They carry armfuls of glorious flowers, many pulled up by the roots, and scores being dropped along the way before being deposited in the car boot. For these people, who have 'enjoyed such a lovely day out in the country', wine making is far more important than the conservation of plants. Similarly with no knowledge even of fundamental woodcraft, the opportunity to see wild creatures is restricted to pure chance, as heavy-footed urban man chatters on about the countryside he came to see and drives wildlife to cover for miles.

I have described elsewhere in this book my first real walk into the heart of Sussex Downland as a child, and its importance to me. It is a walk I have made many times since, both in person and in memory. To some this might seem mere nostalgia, but to me it is far more than that. The moment I walked on to the north slope of Stoke Down and saw, revealed to me in golden sunlight the broad valley fields, the escarpment of Kingley Vale with its Bronze Age bell-barrows, the swooping line of Bow hill, Goodwood and in the distance the main ridge of the South Downs, I knew that I had experienced nothing less than a vision. It was as though high walls had been broken down, a blindfold removed; here indeed was the realisation of a beauty I had suspected but not found before, and through which I knew spirit and imagination could take flight.

Although I have walked in the wildest areas of North America, and experienced the solitude of snow and desert and the grandeur of mountains, the chalk hills of Southern England have remained my favourite walking country. The North and South Downs both have Long Distance Footpaths along them, and being in an area which is very much commuter country they are increasingly used. The South Downs Way reaches from Hampshire across Sussex to Beachy Head and was the country's first long distance bridleway. Many of us now enjoy a day in the country, but a walk of several days' duration is an entirely different experience. There is a sense of real adventure, even though the terrain is not difficult; indeed the chalk turf puts a spring in the step and the very air itself is intoxicating. Having walked the Downs in both directions and in all seasons I find I enjoy travelling from west to east best of all; there is such a satisfying sense of journey's end when arriving at Beachy Head on the Channel coast. No matter which way you walk, however, the noble clump of beech trees known as Chanctonbury Ring, planted by Charles Goring of Wiston two centuries ago, provides what I believe to be the finest panoramic view in the south of England. There is a sensuality that pervades the Downland, a feeling of eternal and beguiling youth and, perhaps because they do not have the impressive majesty and hardness of mountains, we expect less of the Downs and find therefore much more.

The North Downs Way was opened by the Archbishop of Canterbury in 1978. It is the most accessible long distance footpath, being within easy reach of London and extending from Farnham to Dover. My favourite stretch of it is across the Surrey Hills and through the lovely walking country around Dorking. An Ordnance Survey map adds greatly to the enjoyment of any walk in Britain, and there are plenty of guides and information sheets available for all who wish to follow the Long Distance Paths.

Most important of all to the enjoyment of walking is the attitude of the walker. As with any other form of exercise, new walkers are best advised to

The majestic sweep of the Sussex Downs. In the far distance (left) is Chanctonbury Ring, planted two centuries ago and now a welcome landmark for the walker.

start gently. In any case, time is needed during the day to visit some welcoming village, to explore the church, and perhaps to try the local ale. Always it is the journey rather than the arrival that matters, but among many of the foot-weary participants in sponsored walks that I have encountered, this principle seems to be reversed. Walking for real pleasure has nothing to do with large numbers, and when you walk with companions it is best if they are at one with your own outlook, feelings and goals. I find repugnant, to say the least, vast columns of garrulous walkers, clad in army surplus combat jackets and looking like a rabble guerrilla army in a banana republic.

I shall never fail to lift up my eyes unto the hills, and, for as long as I am able, shall walk upon them and speak in their praise.

Highland Ways

TOM WEIR

Mixed feelings assailed me in the mid-seventies, when the plan to make the first Long Distance Walk in Scotland was approved by the Secretary of State for Scotland. My feelings were mixed, not because I did not want others to enjoy the wild east shore of Loch Lomond, the delights of the old Caledonian pinewoods of Loch Tulla, the old road by Ba Bridge to the Devil's Staircase and on over the flanks of the Mamore hills to Fort William; but because, as an old back-packer, I don't like things to be too easy. You may think it selfish of me, but I like my favourite haunts to be well defended by hill-burns, bogs and rocks, or by difficult routes requiring bold map-reading and firm decision-making.

Also, as far as I was concerned there was nothing new about the West Highland Way, since something like fifty miles of its length lay along rights of way already well used by the outdoor fraternity. To link the loose ends needed only a little imagination, and so I thought it rather pompous of the recently formed Countryside Commission for Scotland to describe the proposal as offering '... an important new outdoor recreational opportunity, both for people who wish to use only short lengths as well as those who choose to walk the full route'.

Change and development can take strange paths. Going back to the beginning, the West Highland Way came into recreational use as an escape from urbanism in the mid-thirties, when the first generation of working-class outdoor folk took to the hills. I was one of them, an amateur. The real professionals were the unemployed who kept a fire constantly alight in the Craigallion woods just north of Milngavie.

What I remember about these tough men was their idealism. They travelled light but there would be room for a book of poetry in their packs, and Robert Service was one of their gods.

> *Have you ever been out in the great alone*
> *When the Moon was awful clear,*
> *And the icy mountains hemmed you in,*
> *With a silence you almost could hear ...*

Yes, 'Songs of a Sourdough', and they wanted to be as hard as those men of the Yukon. No tent or paraffin stove for them; they could get a drum-up fire going on the wettest day, make a snug doss under any rock, and live on their meagre rations for three days between the compulsory visits to the Labour Exchange. Round the campfire where they foregathered before returning home there was always laughter and good stories. It was there that I learned about dry caves and empty houses in the hills where I could shelter.

Those still alive are in their seventies now, and they've seen a revolution in working-class outlook and affluence. The Great Outdoors has become an industry, even a necessity, in an age when ordinary folk have more hours of leisure than they know what to do with. Provision for walkers comes within the remit of the Countryside Commission, and it was the absence of any long distance route in Scotland similar to the 1500 miles of such tracks in England and Wales that decided them to do something in the north. The result was the upgrading of the old escape route, trimmed, dressed and waymarked, and called 'The West Highland Way', complete with official guidebook.

Tom Weir prefers the long-established trails of the Highland clansmen to the waymarked formality of the new cross-country routes. 'I'm against taking the wild out of wilderness.'

Even before the first Long Distance Route was established in 1980, two others were on the way, the first starting from Aviemore in the Spey Valley and crossing over moors and forest to the low country where the great river empties into the sea on the Moray Firth.

The second is more ambitious, and cuts right across southern Scotland from Port Patrick near the Mull of Galloway to the Berwickshire coast at Cockburnspath, traversing 204 miles of Lowland country that is by no means low. It begins gently at Port Patrick, then winds into the granite Highlands by Glen Trool and on to the Nith at Sanquhar, climbing to Wanlockhead, the highest village in Scotland, before its descent to Bealtock and Moffat. The next sixty-mile stretch across the hills to Galashiels originated in a resurvey of rights of way by interested naturalists, hill-walkers, family groups, and even a Scottish country dance group who thought it would be a good way to keep fit. The route had been traversed bit by bit and they wanted someone to test it out as a single walk; I had the honour of being invited to be first across and pronounced it excellent. I had only one complaint – the broiling weather. The day we started out was the hottest since records began, and it was nineteen miles of swarming houseflies and torturing thirst since every hill burn was dry. The walk took us three and a half days. The route then continues by Melrose and Gattonside into Lauderdale and the Lammermuirs to where these hills end in the sea at Cockburnspath.

I like the idea of long distance routes opening up new ways for walkers, but I am not so keen on seeing too much refurbishing of long-established old routes with stiles and guideposts and bridges where none were before. I am against taking the wild out of the wilderness, nor do I want to know too exactly how my journey is going to begin and end. Frankly, I abhor guidebooks in the rucksack. I consult them at home against the map, and like to do a bit of background reading about the country where I am going, but then it is time to set out to discover it with the map alone, trying wherever possible to choose the perfect season for the walk. June or October are best for the West Highland Way: early, before the bracken becomes rank; and late, when it complements the brilliant autumn colours.

There are in fact plenty of long distance walks in Scotland that trace right back to the time of the clansmen. The paths may be faint but the rights of way follow natural features, and in these lonely places the map is usually easy to read. For the best of these routes consult the 'District' guides published by the Scottish Mountaineering Trust; there are nine of these, covering the whole of Scotland, and they are obtainable from all booksellers and outdoor equipment suppliers. But please note that on Ordnance Survey sheets covering Scotland, rights of way are not marked as for England and Wales – we like to be different.

Selborne's Hollow Ways

RICHARD MABEY

The village of Selborne in Hampshire is, thanks to the writings of its eighteenth-century curate Gilbert White, probably one of the best known and most frequently visited rural communities in Britain. It has changed very little in the last two hundred years, and in it you can find space to catch your breath and experience a little of what the English landscape must have felt like before the agricultural revolution.

It is really only in its communications with the outside world that Selborne has been transformed. Visitors and residents alike can now travel along the straight and well-appointed B-road between Alton and Liss. If you are on this road it is worth pausing a while, for about half a mile north of the church there is a sharp and symbolic confrontation between the old landscape and the new. Just here, what appears to be an overgrown ditch winds off to the east at right-angles to the road. It is deep and dark, and filled with rocks and modern rubbish. In wet seasons it floods, and acts as an accidental (if very welcome) drainage system for the adjoining farms. But less than a hundred and fifty years ago it carried a very different kind of traffic, for this is the remains of what was once the main highway from Alton. There are dozens of such sunken fragments scattered around the parish, like the hollows left by an abandoned skeleton. They once held the village together, preserving its sense of identity and community, yet also, because of the hazardous conditions that existed on them, its isolation.

Today ease of access has helped add a new economic prosperity to Selborne's traditional charms. Commuters and retired couples now live in the farmworkers' cottages. Container lorries from the flourishing towns nearby thunder through its narrow high street, past the parked cars of visitors who have come to see White's mother-lode first hand. And they in turn have encouraged another kind of local industry, bookshops and craftsmen and sellers of White memorabilia. In this last respect at least, old Selborne has acquired a contemporary meaning that is denied to many similar villages not fortunate enough to have nourished a *genius loci*.

Yet it is a worrying meaning, and not just for those few hundred inhabitants who must sometimes feel swamped by tourists who have come from all over the world. We all fret about such portentous issues as relevance and priority, and about whether we really wish the countryside to be reduced to a museum for old fossils and curates' golden eggs. We would, I think, prefer to find a more lively reconciliation between the new agriculture that is the dominant business of the rural landscape, and the sense of continuity and peace (however illusory) that is the crop we most consciously demand of it; and, at a more immediate level, between the pilgrims, passing through, and the shopping villagers. The poet Edward Thomas had his famous vision of 'all the birds of Oxfordshire and Gloucestershire' from a train that stopped briefly at Adlestrop station. Now we glimpse old England from the windows of a parked car.

At so many levels the crisis of the modern countryside presents itself as a problem of communication between what are, seemingly, 'outsiders' and 'countrymen'. How – and why – to find a way into a foreign village, a fading landscape? How to find a language in which the romantic traveller and the resident realist can explain their needs to each other? They seem peculiarly contemporary dilemmas, yet the same problems, at the same levels, have always been there. It was out of the tension they generated that much of our image of the traditional landscape has been forged.

In the 1820s Selborne was such an isolated community that William Cobbett, who was born and raised just ten miles away in Farnham, had scarcely heard of it and passed it by on the first of his Rural Rides. Fifty years before, when White was working and writing in the village, its hollow ways and 'delug'd paths' were impassable to all but horsemen for much of the year. We can imagine the effect such isolation must have had on this insatiably inquisitive man, hungry for intellectual contact and cursed by coach-sickness. He wrote of the lanes often and seemed to find in them something of the thrill, the challenge and exasperation that he saw in living creatures:

Among the singularities of this place the two rocky hollow lanes, the one to Alton, the other to the forest [Woolmer], deserve our attention. These roads, running through the malm lands, are, by the traffic of the ages, and the fretting of water, worn down through the first stratum of our freestone, and partly through the second; so that they look more like water-courses than roads ... In many places they are reduced sixteen or eighteen feet beneath the level of the fields; and after floods, and in frosts, exhibit very grotesque and wild appearances, from the tangled roots that are twisted among the strata, and from the torrents rushing down their broken sides; and especially when those cascades are frozen into icicles, hanging in all the fanciful shapes of frostwork. These rugged gloomy scenes affright the ladies when they peep down into them from the paths above, and make timid horsemen shudder while they ride along them; but delight the naturalist with their various botany, and particularly with their curious *filices* [ferns] with which they abound.

Whoever the 'timid horsemen' were, White was certainly not amongst them. He was out in the lanes in all weathers, doing his parish duties and collecting notes for his book, even when conditions were as bad as they were in the notorious winter of 1776. He writes in his journal for 14 January:

Rugged, Siberian weather. The narrow lanes are full of snow in some places, which is driven into most romantic and grotesque shapes. The road-waggons are obliged to stop, and the stage-coaches are much embarrassed. I was obliged to be much abroad on this day, and scarce ever saw its fellow.

In fact he was to see equally violent weather many times over the succeeding years. On 5 June 1784, Selborne was struck by a localised storm of unprecedented violence. It was presaged, White recalls, by 'a blue mist, smelling strongly of sulphur, hanging along our sloping woods, and seeming to indicate that thunder was at hand'. Then came hail and convex pieces of ice, three inches across, which broke all the windows on the north side of his house:

We were just sitting down to dinner; but were soon diverted from our repast by the clattering of tiles and the jingling of glass. There fell at the same time prodigious torrents of rain on the farms ... which occasioned a flood as violent as it was sudden; doing great damage to the meadows and fallows, by deluging the one and washing away the soil of the other. The hollow lane towards Alton was so torn and disordered as not to be passable until mended, rocks being removed that weighed 200 weight. Those that saw the effect which the great hail had on ponds and pools say that the dashing of the water made an extraordinary appearance, the froth and spray standing up in the air three feet above the surface. The rushing and roaring of the hail, as it approached, was truly tremendous.

The hollow ways, alternately worn down and blocked off, sculptured by frost, flood, traffic and the labours of the beleaguered villagers, were (and still are) a geological record of Selborne's history. In the manner of an archaeological dig, the deeper they sank the more they revealed of the parish's experience. In White's writings they came to be almost a symbol of his own ambivalent history, as an intellectually precocious and socially progressive curate, who was confined by his own choice in a remote Hampshire village. Perhaps the block they represented to his gregarious nature was partly responsible for the energy he threw into correspondence and journal writing. (His life-long friend John Mulso, who lived just ten miles to the south-west in Meonstoke, once wrote to him, 'I have two great griefs: one that I cannot ride; the other that you are accessible by no other vehicle ... I should not care a halfpenny about the road to Selborne, if I had not a regard to Etty and a love for you.') And perhaps the catastrophic storm of 1784 was some kind of watershed for him, as it clearly was for the village. At any rate he seemed pleased with the repairs that were made to the local lanes that autumn, which enabled a coach to enter the village along the direct western approach for the first time ever on 23 November.

On this occasion, at least, White's fascination with the capricious wildness of the lanes took second place to his concern for the villagers' welfare. Many of the other trackways that criss-cross the parish – the Zig-zag that tacks up the hanging beechwood, for instance, and the Bostal, cut more gradually across it – were built under his instructions, as much for their benefit as his own. And it was concern about the villagers' interests over that persistently troubled network of lanes to the north-west of the village that produced one of his last references to the parish highways. It was in the autumn of 1789, four years before his death. The tide of Parliamentary enclosure was rising in the district and an ambitious local farmer had closed off an ancient trackway up near Northfield Hill. When one of the village's oldest citizens took direct action to re-open the right of way, Selbourne's vigilant curate lent a hand.

> Be it remembered that there had been from time immemorial an undisputed bridle road from the east corner of the north field, across Bushy plot and along the south end of Norton mead and the north end of Yfremead, and across the seven acres into the hollow stony lane leading to Norton farm – till about the year 1770, when Sir Simeon Stuart at the instance of farmer Young, then his tenant at Norton farm, ordered the abovesaid road to be shut up and so deprived the neighbourhood of the advantage of that way: but now, in 1787, Mr Hammond senior, aged 81, of Newton great farm, but till late of Little Ward-le-ham, demanded a passage for himself and horse, of which he and others have made use the summer thro': nor has farmer Richard Knight, the present tenant of Norton farm, made any objection to what has been done ... This account was written by Gilbert White, an ancient inhabitant and native of Selborne, on Sept 22nd 1789.

The last written record we have of the hollow lanes being actually in use is from the 1830s. Edward Blythe, doing fieldwork for his introduction to an 1836 edition of the *Natural History*, decided to try and get a White's-eye

Above: A reproduction from an early edition of the Natural History.

Below: These cottages at Longstock in Hampshire preserve the character of the time White was living and working in the area.

view of the local scenery by coming in on the Old Alton Road. He all but turned over his coach in the boulder-strewn track, and on his next visit walked by footpath, at ground level. The route he followed was the one adopted for the new Alton road, built some fifteen years later.

Landscapes do not just feature in historical accounts, they are direct historical records in their own right. Yet it is impossible to divide the two meanings. When a writer or artist 'captures' – it is such an apt description – a landscape, he changes its future. If the place helps form the writer, the writer in turn helps conserve the place, by directing our attention more acutely to its character. There are in Britain many patches of countryside as anciently etched as Selborne, unobserved and only dimly understood because they had no celebratory voice. But where we can read, so to speak, the place of the book, we can see through two pairs of eyes, and begin to understand that ancient landscapes are, in Margaret Drabble's words, 'a link between what we were and what we are'.

Yet it is perhaps an overbearing concern with what has gone before that most bedevils our relationship with the countryside today. It is understandable that we look to the rural landscape for an echo of a less troubled past, in the world or in our own childhoods, yet sad that we so often fail to recognise the points of continuity between the old world and the new. A sense of vague but all pervading loss has been the dominant mood of countryside writing for the last hundred years. A. E. Housman, writing of his 'blue remembered hills' in Shropshire, called them

> ... the land of lost content,
> I see it shining plain, the happy highways where I went
> And cannot come again.

But Selborne's ancient highways are one place we can come to again, and in a spirit more of honest rediscovery than of pastoral fantasy. Although we can use them as cool retreats and enjoy the same flowers and 'curious *filices*' as grew there two hundred years ago, they are also uncompromising evidence of the mixed fortunes of a millennium of parish life.

I have often wondered if it might be possible to clear out the drainage pipes and the rubbish of a century and re-open what remains of the hollow ways for public use. I am not thinking of some signposted pleasure trail ('Follow in the Reverend's footsteps') but a rough and ready alternative system for walkers and riders. I do not think it would matter whether this were done for the sake of those curious about White or their own histories, or simply for those anxious to escape the juggernaut lorries on the new road. One would be a way back, the other a way forward, but they would share a common concern for the human meaning of landscapes.

I think White understood the crucial link that landscapes can provide when they are allowed to evolve. In a short, undated, epigrammatic poem, quite unlike the conventionally formal verse he usually wrote, he expresses what I think may have been his private feelings about the road improvements he publicly applauded. It is called 'On a Bad Road, Ill Mended':

> Cramm'd up with furze, with faggots, and huge stones,
> What a rough road of glass, hards, flints, and bones!
> Blockheads are always busy'd in the wrong;
> Mend not at all and one might get along.

Key to
Victorian Hand Tools

1 Costrel These little barrels made of oak and hooped with iron, also called harvest bottles, were used by farmworkers to carry cider and beer into the fields.

2 Traveller The traveller was an important tool of the wheelwright's craft. Made in either metal or wood, it measured the circumference of a wheel so that the iron tyre could be cut to the exact length required. The tyre, while still hot, was then shrunk on to the wheel for a perfect fit.

3 Corn Measure This provided an accurate measure – usually half a gallon – of corn or other cereals more quickly than conventional scales.

4 Horn Cups These drinking vessels were made from sections of cow horn and were the common drinking cups of the country labourer.

5 Jerry This claw-like instrument was used by wool-staplers to hold the sides of a packed sheet or bale together so that it could be fastened more easily.

6 Whimbel A gadget for twisting straw or hay into lengths of rope or bonds, used for example in rick-thatching.

7 Bale Hook These hooks were pushed into the sides of a bale or sack, usually of wool, to provide a hand-hold for easier lifting.

8 Butter Scoop Shovel-like butter scoops like this were to be found in every Victorian dairy and kitchen. The chip-carved handle was also used to apply a 'print' decoration to the butter after it had been scooped from the churn.

9 Bark Scraper (or Tan Spud) An instrument for stripping the bark from felled trees; the bark was then sold to the tanyards.

10 Bird Scarer This rattle, similar to those later used by policemen, air-raid wardens and football fans, was first used by young children for driving birds away from planted fields.

Countryside Organisations

Countryside organisations can be divided into two types – statutory or official bodies and non-statutory or voluntary bodies. The statutory organisations are established and financed by the government, although they often have considerable independence of action. The non-statutory organisations consist of the numerous trusts, clubs and societies concerned with country matters, and are often registered charities. Although they are predominantly voluntary, the larger ones are also able to employ paid staff. The following lists are by no means exhaustive but indicate some of the different aspects of the organisations.

Statutory Organisations

Countryside Commission   *Headquarters: John Dower House, Crescent Place, Cheltenham, Gloucestershire GL50 3RA (also regional offices in England and Wales; The Countryside Commission for Scotland, Battleby House, Redgorton, Perth)*
The Countryside Commission is an independent statutory body whose aim is the enhancement of the landscape in England and Wales and the provision and improvement of facilities for the enjoyment of the countryside. It has also replaced and taken over the functions of the National Parks Commission in dealing with national parks, areas of outstanding natural beauty, heritage coasts, long distance routes, country parks and picnic sites.

The Forestry Commission   *Headquarters: 231 Corstorphine Rd, Edinburgh EH12 7AT (also regional offices)*
The Forestry Commission is responsible for establishing and maintaining forests and for promoting the interests of forestry and the production and supply of timber in Britain. It also has a duty under the Countryside Acts to help conserve the natural beauty and amenity of the countryside.

The Nature Conservancy Council   *Headquarters: 19 Belgrave Square, London SW1X 8PY (also regional offices)*
The Nature Conservancy Council is the official body responsible for the conservation of the countryside in Britain. The NCC advises government, both nationally and locally, as well as public bodies, landowners and all those whose activities affect the countryside and its wildlife. It establishes, maintains and manages National Nature Reserves.

Non-Statutory Organisations

The Society for the Promotion of Nature Conservation *Headquarters: The Green, Nettleham, Lincolnshire LN2 2NR*

SPNC is the national association of the Nature Conservation Trusts, promoting and assisting the work being carried out by the Trusts and also initiating projects and advising on land acquisition. It acts as a focal point for national conservation issues. SPNC is also closely involved with the running of Watch, the national environmental club for young people, and the junior branch of the Nature Conservation Trusts.

Nature Conservation Trusts

The Trusts are a nationwide network of 42 organisations concerned with all aspects of nature conservation at a local level. All are associated with the Society for the Promotion of Nature Conservation and, incidentally, all are registered charities.

1. England and Wales

Avon Wildlife Trust, *17 Whiteladies Rd, Bristol B28 1PB*
Bedfordshire and Huntingdonshire Naturalists' Trust, *38 Mill St, Bedford MK40 3HD*
Berkshire, Buckinghamshire and Oxfordshire Naturalists' Trust, *122 Church Way, Iffley, Oxford OX4 4EG*
Brecknock County Naturalists' Trust, *Chapel House, Llechfaen, Brecon, Powys*
Cambridgeshire and Isle of Ely Naturalists' Trust, *1 Brookside, Cambridge CB2 1JF*
Cheshire Conservation Trust, *c/o Marbury Country Park, Northwich CW9 6AT*
Cornwall Naturalists' Trust, *Trendrine, Zennor, St Ives TR26 3BW*
Cumbria Naturalists' Trust, *Rydal Rd, Ambleside LA22 9AN*
Derbyshire Naturalists' Trust, *Estate Office, Twyford, Barrow-on-Trent DE7 1HJ*
Devon Trust for Nature Conservation, *75 Queen St, Exeter*
Dorset Naturalists' Trust, *39 Christchurch Rd, Bournemouth*
Durham County Conservation Trust, *52 Old Elvet, Durham DH1 3HN*
Essex Naturalists' Trust, *Fingringhoe Wick Nature Reserve, South Green Rd, Fingringhoe, Colchester CO5 7DN*
Glamorgan Naturalists' Trust, *104 Broadway, Cowbridge CF7 7EY*
Gloucestershire Trust for Nature Conservation, *Church House, Standish, Stonehouse GL10 3EU*
Gwent Trust for Nature Conservation, *c/o College of Agriculture, Usk*
Hampshire and Isle of Wight Naturalists' Trust, *8 Market Place, Romsey SO5 8WB*
Herefordshire and Radnorshire Nature Trust, *25 Castle St, Hereford HR1 2NW*
Hertfordshire and Middlesex Trust for Nature Conservation, *Offley Place, Great Offley, Hitchin SG5 3DS*
Kent Trust for Nature Conservation, *PO Box 29, Maidstone ME14 1XH*
Lancashire Naturalists' Trust, *Dale House, Dale Head, Slaidburn*
Leicestershire and Rutland Trust for Nature Conservation, *1 West St, Leicester LE1 6UU*

Lincolnshire and South Humberside Trust for Nature Conservation, *The Manor House, Alford LN13 9DL*

Norfolk Naturalists' Trust, *72 Cathedral Close, Norwich NR1 4DF*

Northamptonshire Naturalists' Trust, *Lings House, Billing Lings, Northampton NN3 4BE*

Northumberland Wildlife Trust, *Hancock Museum, Barras Bridge, Newcastle-upon-Tyne NE2 4PT*

North Wales Naturalists' Trust, *154 High St, Bangor, Gwynedd LL57 1NU*

Nottinghamshire Trust for Nature Conservation, *110 Mansfield Rd, Nottingham NG1 3HL*

Shropshire Conservation Trust, *Bear Steps, Shrewsbury SY1 1UH*

Somerset Trust for Nature Conservation, *Fyne Court, Broomfield, Bridgwater TA5 2EQ*

Staffordshire Nature Conservation Trust, *3a Newport Rd, Stafford*

Suffolk Trust for Nature Conservation, *St Peter's House, Cutler St, Ipswich IP1 1UU*

Surrey Trust for Nature Conservation, *Tunbarr Garden Cottage, Headley, Epsom KT18 6PQ*

Sussex Trust for Nature Conservation, *Woods Mill, Henfield BN5 9SD*

Warwickshire Nature Conservation Trust, *Northgate, Warwick CV34 4PB*

West Wales Naturalists' Trust, *7 Market St, Haverfordwest, Dyfed*

Wiltshire Trust for Nature Conservation, *4 Peppercombe Close, Urchfont, Devizes SN10 4QS*

Worcestershire Nature Conservation Trust, *The Lodge, Beacon Lane, Rednal, Birmingham B45 9XN*

Yorkshire Naturalists' Trust, *20 Castlegate, York YO1 1RP*

2. Scotland

Scottish Wildlife Trust, *8 Dublin St, Edinburgh EH1 3PP*

3. Northern Ireland

Ulster Trust for Nature Conservation, *Inver Cottage, 67 Huntley Rd, Banbridge, County Down*

4. Isle of Man

Manx Nature Conservation Trust, *Ivie Cottage, Kirk Michael, Isle of Man*

Council for the Protection of Rural England   *Headquarters: 4 Hobart Place, London SW1 0HY*

The Council exists to protect all that is worth while in the English countryside while recognising that change is often necessary and can be for the good. The CPRE concerns itself with developments such as new housing, power stations, reservoirs, sand and gravel workings, the felling and planting of trees, and the siting of new roads and motorways. It lobbies MPs and advises government departments. There are branches in most counties and similar organisations in Scotland and Wales.

National Trust   *Headquarters: 42 Queen Anne's Gate, London SW1H 9AS (also regional offices)*

The National Trust acquires and maintains not only buildings of architectural or historic interest, but also much open countryside.

Royal Society for the Protection of Birds   *Headquarters: The Lodge, Sandy, Bedfordshire (also regional offices)*
The RSPB is concerned with all aspects of wild bird conservation, and owns and manages some very important nature reserves.

Wildfowl Trust   *Headquarters: Slimbridge, Gloucestershire*
The Trust is concerned with all aspects of wildfowl conservation and has wildfowl refuges at Slimbridge and elsewhere in the country.

In addition to organisations such as those above, in which land management figures prominently, there are many specialised societies and organisations which promote the welfare and study of particular species or particular fields of interest. Some examples of these are the Botanical Society of the British Isles, the British Trust for Ornithology, the British Deer Society, and many more; unfortunately space does not permit the publication of a full list. There are also countless local natural history and archaeological societies and field clubs throughout Britain.

Some organisations which involve active participation on the part of their members are:

British Trust for Conservation Volunteers   *Headquarters: 10–14 Duke St, Reading, Berkshire (also regional offices)*
The BTCV is a national organisation with many local branches, whose members carry out a variety of conservation tasks in their spare time. Its aim is nature conservation through practical work and it is of great assistance to the Nature Conservation Trusts and other organisations.

Ramblers' Association   *Headquarters: 1–4 Crawford Mews, York St, London W1H 1PT*
The aim of the Ramblers' Association is to protect the interests of ramblers, maintaining and extending their rights and privileges, while encouraging friendly relations with landowners and the rural community generally.

Youth Hostels' Association   *Headquarters: Trevelyan House, 8 St Stephen's Hill, St Albans, Hertfordshire*
The aim of the Association is to help everyone of limited means, especially young people, to a greater knowledge, love and care of the countryside by providing cheap and convenient accommodation.

Field Studies Council   *Headquarters: Preston Montford, Montford Bridge, Shrewsbury, Shropshire SY4 1HW*
The interests of the Field Studies Council are primarily educational: to promote a better understanding of the environment. It manages ten field centres in England and Wales at which are run short residential courses.

Index

Numbers in italic refer to illustrations

Picture Acknowledgements

Aerofilms Ltd: **71, 72, 74, 79.** By permission of the Ashmolean Museum: **72** (inserts). BBC Copyright: **3, 5, 8, 51, 61, 89, 142** below, **156.** Gordon Beningfield: vi, **41, 90, 102, 154, 159, 172, 195.** Thomas Bewick, *A History of British Birds* Vols I and II (1826): **161, 163, 164.** British Tourist Authority: **21.** Countryside Commission /photograph Leonard and Marjorie Gayton: **185,** Peter Crawford: **52, 53, 140** above, **142** above, **175–8.** Danby Lodge, North York Moors National Park Centre: **182.** Phil Drabble: **18.** Geg Germany: **48, 49, 54, 139.** Courtesy Holland and Holland Ltd/photographs Chris Dawes: **92, 93.** Eric Hosking: **45** below (insert). D. G. Johnson: **17.** Mansell Collection: **67** below, **81.** Michael J. Martin: **131.** National Trust: **171.** Howard Payton: **57, 118, 122, 124.** A. E. Mc.R. Pearce: **22.** Bernard Price: **84, 133.** University of Reading, Institute of Agricultural History and Museum of English Rural Life: **67** above, **108, 126, 129, 132.** Angela Rippon: **45** below. Jim Saunders: **45** above. Scottish Wildlife Trust/photograph C. K. Mylne: **29.** F. M. Slater: **30.** Sussex Trust for Nature Conservation: **31.** Tate Gallery, London: **140** below, **141** above. James Thomson, *The Seasons* (1777): **111.** John Topham Picture Library: **193** below. Lee Weatherley: **141** below. Tom Weir: **96, 97** left, **103–6, 187.** Rev. Gilbert White, *Natural History and Antiquities of Selborne*: ii, **193** above. Barclay Wills: **158.**